Live!

AT THE

ozark opry

DAN WILLIAM PEEK
Foreword by Joyce Mace

**Missouri Center
for the Book**

**Missouri Authors
Collection**

Charleston   London

THE
History
PRESS

Published by The History Press
Charleston, SC 29403
www.historypress.net

First published 2010

Manufactured in the United States

ISBN 978.1.59629.098.3

Library of Congress Cataloging-in-Publication Data

Peek, Dan William.
Live! at the Ozark Opry / Dan William Peek.
p. cm.
Includes bibliographical references.
ISBN 978-1-59629-098-3
1. Ozark Opry. 2. Country music--History and criticism. I. Title.
ML3524.P44 2010
781.64209778'56--dc22
2010039381

CONTENTS

CONTENTS

FOREWORD

I want to take this opportunity to thank everyone for the support and kindness my husband, Lee Mace, and I have received over the years and for the ongoing interest in the Ozark Opry.

From the very beginning, we enjoyed doing the show, working with so many fine musicians and entertainers and meeting and visiting with people from all over the country and all over the world.

The single most important thing that I found out over the years is that every challenge brings with it an opportunity. When we lost Lee, it was hard to go on, but we did, for twenty more years. When Bill Atterberry decided to take some time off after so many years with the show—that was hard. But it gave a young entertainer, Matt Gumm, a chance to work with the show. There were many more challenges and rewards in the time of the Ozark Opry. All are wonderful memories now.

I am sometimes asked how Lee and I put together a country show that ran continually for fifty-three years. I think Lee had a good answer to that question. He said it in an interview many years ago:

> *Our intent has always been good. The music can vary, the style can vary, the songs can vary. But our intent has always been that when they walk in here and give their time or spend their money to come here our intent is that they must have a good time...That has always been our intent—Always.*

Joyce Mace

ACKNOWLEDGEMENTS

I regret that space does not allow me to thank all of the many folks who helped with this book. Please know that all are appreciated.

As always, I am grateful to my wife, Joy, my daughter, Sarah, and her husband, Tom, for their editing advice and patience. A special notice is due to the Ozark Opry's Jim Phinney and to Dr. Joe Pryor of the Miller County Historical Society for their invaluable research assistance. Thanks to Ben Gibson and Jaime Muehl, my editors at The History Press, for their guidance and expertise. To Dr. Howard W. Marshall, my profound thanks for direction on the writing when I strayed. And to Joyce Mace, whose strength and spirit are an inspiration, for granting me access to the memorabilia and memories that were crucial in bringing this important story to print—I am more than grateful.

INTRODUCTION

In 1962, when I was a junior in high school in Versailles, Missouri, two schoolmates, Ken Peoples and Jerome Wheeler, and I formed a musical group, patterned on the popular folk singers the Kingston Trio. Because Ken could play guitar and Jerome the mandolin, I was assigned the task of learning to play banjo. I purchased a banjo—an old open-back frailing banjo—for five dollars, rescued from the attic of someone in town, and set about learning the instrument.

This casual foray into music would lead me to meet and spend a fair amount of time with Lee Mace between the fall of 1963 and the fall of 1964—my eighteenth year on the planet.

Lee hired the three of us, the New Morning Singers, to perform in Lee Mace's Hillbilly Hootenanny. He sent us home from the talent show with instructions to make a microphone and stand from a broom handle, a wooden Christmas tree stand and a Cracker Jack box. We were to practice moving in and out of the microphone as we played and sang. This was our introduction to professional entertainment. There would be much more tutoring to come. We appeared numerous times on the *Ozark Opry* television show, and Lee booked several performances for us at fairs and events that year.

But for the most part, our duties were to perform at the hootenanny in the evening and then rush up the street to do one number on the Ozark Opry stage to promote the hootenanny show. That number was usually the campaign song of old-time Missouri politician Champ Clark: "Every Time I Go to Town, the Boys Keep Kicking My Dog Around." Lee liked that tune.

In 2003, I met with Joyce Mace to ask for her blessing for this book. Based on a lengthy interview with Joyce, I began preliminary research. As I linked the names and dates of the story to the lives and careers of Lee and Joyce, the broader context and importance of the Ozark Opry emerged.

Lee and Joyce Mace not only succeeded in Nashville as country music artists, but also in the process they decoded the country music industry formula and then created an alternative business model, which is now generally termed "Branson-style" entertainment.

1

ONCE UPON A TIME IN THE OZARKS

The Ozark Opry auditorium still looms beside Highway 54 in Osage Beach, Missouri. In front of the structure, a few yards off the highway pavement, the giant curved arrow sign continues to beckon traffic into the parking lot as it has for nearly a half century. But the lot is a fraction of the five-hundred-car capacity of the Ozark Opry's heyday, and it may eventually be further overrun as the once rural byway swells to an urban expressway.

Gone is the show's closing announcement: "Thanks for 53 Great Years— Joyce Mace," which graced the marquee sign beneath the giant arrow a couple of years after the stage went silent. But a mile or so in either direction of the Ozark Opry are signs designating this stretch of highway as the Lee Mace Memorial Highway.

Inside the auditorium, 829 threadbare seats face the stage, still expectant of a show. The concession booth to the left of the stage stands abandoned, its "Snak Bar" sign (with the N backward) a symbol of the beginnings of Lee Mace's Ozark Opry.

But a hint of magic remains. Multitudes of people across the nation remember the spell cast from this stage. They know they would be swept up in it again if they could walk through the doors once more and hear Lee Mace, leaning forward from his bass fiddle, call from the stage, "How many of you folks came here tonight to have a good time?" Also on stage they would see the upright piano with thumbtacks driven into the hammer pads to give it a tinny old-time sound, five-string banjo and fiddle music and "Goofer," the beloved country comedian of the show. Everybody came to the Ozark Opry to have a good time.

And what a good time it was.

An Ozark Opry ticket line, 1959. The original sign and Rural Highway 54 are in the background. *Courtesy Joyce Mace.*

This is the true tale of how, by holding steadfast to traditional country music and values, Lee and Joyce Mace established a remarkable entertainment enterprise that changed for the better the lives of many of those it touched, an enterprise that for over five decades delighted generations upon generations of visitors to the Lake of the Ozarks and created a successful alternative to the corporate music entertainment industry in America.

It may seem improbable, but this vibrant story begins in a humble potato field in the state of Washington.

Dating at least to the days of the Great Depression, in the pre-mechanized era of potato harvesting, a custom—a rite of passage—for young men from the Ozark Mountains of Missouri was a trek to the Northwest Territory seeking seasonal employment rooting out and boxing up potatoes.

Every year, the boys from Miller and Camden Counties headed for Wapato, Washington. Post-Depression potato growers there had come to rely on German prisoners of war and interned Japanese Americans for labor during World War II. Then the war ended, and peace brought a labor shortage.

So it was that two youths of the Ozarks, Lee Mace and Carl Williams, who hailed from Miller County and Camden County, respectively, found themselves, in 1946, side by side in the fields of Wapato, engaged in the grueling labor of digging, boxing and sorting potatoes by hand.

Once Upon a Time in the Ozarks

They had not met before, although their home counties adjoined. Lee was just off a year of service in the navy, and Carl was just out of high school. It is very probable that the two immediately discovered that they had much in common—starting with the Ozarks and the customs and traditions of the mountains.

Carl's father was a fiddle player who performed at home for the benefit of his wife and three sons and daughter. All the Williams family members were accomplished jig dancers. Carl's sister recalled that the family would dance at night by the light of a lamp and watch their shadows on the wall as a means of developing and perfecting their jig techniques. She also recollected that her father never played the fiddle outside the home; he played only for those private family dances.

Lee was a guitar player and also an accomplished jig dancer. He would, however, in later years readily concede that Carl was the better dancer.

Jig dancing was a valued skill in the Ozarks at that time. When an organization or club announced a "dance" event, it meant they would be dancing the "Ozark jig," or as Lee Mace called, it the "Ozark Mountain jig."

The Ozark Mountain jig is unique to the Ozarks and is more closely derived from the Irish jig than the clog dancing of the rural South, the buck dancing of the Appalachians or western-style square dancing.

Carl Williams's sister said that everyone in the Ozarks of those days knew how to dance the jig. "It was just something you knew," she said.

As August approached, Lee returned home from the Wapato fields. Carl stayed behind until potato season's end to earn a few more dollars. But the two Ozark men had become close friends—a friendship that would last a lifetime.

Well into the twentieth century, Ozark communities and organizations sponsored carnival and fair-like festivities called picnics. These were usually two- to four-day affairs, although some would go on for up to six days. They were anchored by a dance floor, the lumber for which was often rented, and an Ozarks dance band.

Each year, the Town of Tuscumbia, the seat of Miller County, Missouri, sponsored a huge such event that drew folks from all over the region. The three-day Tuscumbia Picnic was not to be missed. All the politicians and would-be politicians of the region were there, as were nearly all the inhabitants of the surrounding mountains. There were carnival rides and food vendors. A spacious railed-in dance floor was laid, and the best local fiddle bands played each night. It was the social event of the year in the North Central Ozarks.

It follows naturally that Lee Mace was among a large group of young adults from the region who converged upon the Tuscumbia Picnic in 1946.

Joyce Mace's (at right) first job, the Hot Fish restaurant, later Joe Boer's Potted Steer, Osage Beach. *Courtesy Joyce Mace.*

It also follows that the confluence of so much youthful energy would flow onto the dance floor.

The dance floor railing was intended to ensure containment and control of the dancers. But Lee was already on the dance floor when he spied the young lady he hoped to have as his dancing partner that night, and nothing would get in the way of his dancing with her. Her name was Joyce, and she was standing by the railing among a thicket of young men and women observing the dance. One of Lee's fellow Wapato pilgrims, Burley Wilson, was standing nearby. Carl Williams had not yet returned from the potato harvest.

In a gesture that should inspire awe in, or at least be truly admired by, awkward young men of any era, Lee strode across the vast dance floor, leaned over the railing and offered his hands to the young lady. She accepted, and with an assist from Burley, Lee lifted her over the railing and onto the dance floor.

The young lady and Lee jig danced until the band retired for the evening. After arranging for her friends to drive her car back to her parents' house, Joyce accepted Lee's offer of a ride to the same destination.

Four years later, in 1950, Lee and Joyce—who it so happened was Carl Williams's sister—were married.

Lee, Joyce and Carl had by then become engaged in a successful entertainment enterprise, and it is doubtful that they ever again gave much thought to potato harvesting. They would be far too busy.

This narrative is, to a great extent, a study of a rare marriage of equal partners in life and business—Lee and Joyce Mace. Their story is inextricable from its setting, the Ozark Mountains, the saga of Bagnell Dam and the Lake of the Ozarks and the history of the modern country music industry.

2

THE OZARKS OF OLD

The bands that played the 1946 Tuscumbia Picnic were fiddle bands, which is to say that the fiddler played the melody line while the other instruments played either backup chords or supporting musical configurations, with some, depending on the nature of the instrument, occasionally stepping up to play the melody along with the fiddle. But the fiddler or fiddlers usually owned the melody line. Other than a fiddle, there was no standard instrumentation for the music of the Ozarks of those days. It is quite likely that a piano graced the dance floor at Tuscumbia, and it's entirely possible that a tenor banjo or ukulele was in evidence.

What is certain is that the music of Lee and Joyce Mace's youth was tunes that most Ozark natives of today would be whistling familiar with: "Rag Time Annie," "Redwing" and, if needed for a change-up, the waltz favorite of generations of Missouri fiddlers, "Over the Waves." Most of the Ozark Mountain jig musical tradition consists of versions of Scottish and Irish bagpipe music that the fiddle and banjo translated into American hoedown or "breakdown" music.

Following the Louisiana Purchase, mountain families from Tennessee and Kentucky, many of Scottish or Irish ancestry, began settling the Missouri Ozarks. It is likely that these pioneers put down new roots in the landscape that reminded them most of the eastern mountain ranges from whence they had come. These newcomers joined the sparse population of earlier pioneers and French, Spanish and Native Americans who ranged the Ozarks at that time. The area of the mountains where the Lake of the Ozarks now exists was in those days the habitat of the Osage tribe. Both Lee and Joyce Mace's families are of significant Osage stock.

Lee Mace with his
sister Lois, circa 1930.
Courtesy Joyce Mace.

The Ozark settlers were mostly of a southern tradition, sharing much with that of the neighboring "Little Dixie" culture of north central Missouri. But the Ozarks culture was not so much of the plantation. Put simply, the Ozarker's identity was founded in the knowledge and belief that only those who did for themselves what needed to be done—and who were at least as stubborn as the rocky soil of the mountains—could share their life and kinship and the pride they took in the life and kin of the mountains. This stubborn pride is evident even now in many native Ozarkers—most other attitudes have either been bred out or moved on.

Early Ozarkers were proud of their, or their forebears', service in the War of Independence.

Several counties of the state of Missouri are named for Revolutionary War heroes. Missourians to this day are quick to point out that Little Dixie's Lincoln County is not so named due to Abraham Lincoln; rather, it honors the Continental army general Benjamin Lincoln.

In the Three County area of the northern Ozark Mountains—the setting of this story and often referred to by elder natives as "This Country"—Morgan County is named for another Revolutionary War general, Daniel Morgan.

Missouri Ozarkers are as proud of their ancestors who fought one another in the American Civil War as they are of their Revolutionary War heritage. The battle flag of the Confederacy is seen more than occasionally on rural flagpoles.

In Versailles, Missouri, Morgan County's seat, the graves of Confederate veterans are, on Memorial Day, designated by miniature Confederate battle flags. (Union soldiers each receive a miniature Old Glory.) Local historians Bill and Dorothy Williams, who have indexed the occupants of cemeteries in the county, said that the tally of Union and secessionist dead contained within is about equal.

"Missouri was in the middle in the war," stated Bill Williams. "It seems to have been pretty evenly split around here."

Tapping this Missouri heritage in promotion of the Ozark Opry, Lee Mace frequently printed show advertisements on replicas of the Confederate and Missouri bank notes that circulated during the Civil War.

Confederate reenactors, Versailles, Memorial Day weekend 2010. *Photo by Joy Peek.*

A traveler in the region may from time to time hear tales, surely apocryphal, of old cemeteries deep in the Ozarks in which the Union dead are buried facing north and Confederates facing south.

If the traveler should tarry, other tales will emerge. The sure-footed mule will be celebrated. Ernest McNeil, a longtime associate of Lee Mace, was an Ozarker born in the Indian Territory in 1900. McNeil once noted, "If a man had a good mule, he was ready for anything."

It is useful to be aware, too, of the subtle sense of humor that is reflected in Ozark speech. Irony abounds, and origins are usually unknown.

An expression once favored by Lee Mace to describe an outstanding instrumental performance was that it was "plumb seldom."

Reflecting a past when barter was a part of the region's economy, the redundancy "cash-money" is still often heard.

It is quite true that some Ozarkers of the old days were bootleggers who manufactured the raw whiskey generically known as moonshine. M.R. "Doc" Foster, another longtime friend of Lee Mace, born in 1909 a few miles north of Old Linn Creek and well known in his lifetime as a raconteur and colorful character, recollected that moonshine sold for four dollars a gallon in 1934.

What is not widely known is that many folks in the region used moonshine in a medicinal tonic, which, taken often, could ward off just about any illness and for sure keep evil spirits or haunts at bay. Bill Williams—born in the mid-1920s—related that this elixir was brewed by soaking a handful of the roots of a weed known as poke in a quart or so of moonshine. Pokeroot taken alone is deadly poisonous.

Before the construction of Bagnell Dam, which created the Lake of the Ozarks and resulting tourism and vacation homes on the shoreline, the mountains of the Three County area were isolated and only infrequently visited by the city folk of St. Louis and Kansas City.

Those from the city who visited the area were often wealthy business owners who visualized living grandly in the picturesque Ozarks as country squires. Some even acted on the dream. Perhaps the most famous of these was Kansas City's Robert McClure Snyder. Snyder purchased five thousand acres in an area known as Ha Ha Tonka and, in 1905, began building a castle on a high point with a breathtaking panorama about five miles southwest of present-day Camdenton.

The stone castle was built according to authentic old European construction processes and was three and a half stories in height. There were a number of greenhouses, a stone water tower and a stable. Snyder did not live to see the

Ha Ha Tonka Castle. *Missouri State Archives.*

completion of the castle, however; he was killed in a car accident in Kansas City—said to be one of the first such fatalities in Missouri—in 1906.

The Snyder family finally completed the work in 1922. But in 1942, a fireplace spark ignited the structure, and it was gutted completely in the blaze that followed.

In 1978, the State of Missouri purchased the estate, thirty-six hundred acres and the remaining stone walls—only the eighty-foot-tall stone water tower escaped the fire—and opened it to the public as Ha Ha Tonka State Park.

The dream of becoming a country squire in the Ozarks seems to have been a perilous one. The story of Robert McClure Snyder is eerily reflected in another such saga: that of St. Louis real estate mogul Cyrus Crane Willmore, whose story will be related further along.

3

THAT MOUNTAIN MUSIC

For native Ozarkers, the mountains are ancient hymns, tropes of time and timelessness, the immediate and the infinite, constant harmony.

Everything Ozark, from daily life to the legacy of history, is framed in music. By way of example, a standard selection of Missouri fiddlers is "Marmaduke's Hornpipe." Renowned Missouri fiddler and scholar Dr. Howard W. Marshall tells its history in liner notes to his 2001 CD, *Fiddling Missouri*:

> *Oral tradition says it is named for Confederate Gen. John S. Marmaduke, from a dynasty of Little Dixie tobacco and hemp farmers, slave holders, and politicians. He's famous for helping lose the Battle of Boonville in June 1862, a small but key skirmish that gave the Federals control of the Missouri River when the outgunned, outnumbered Rebels beat a disorganized rapid retreat. Marmaduke's father M.M. had been Missouri governor before the war, and John S. was voted into the same chair after Reconstruction.*

Another example from *Fiddling Missouri* is the "Tie Hacker Hoedown." This tune celebrates the occupation followed by many Ozarkers in the nineteenth and well into the twentieth centuries of felling trees from which to fashion railroad ties and then floating the product downriver as rafts to be used in railroad construction and maintenance. The tie hackers are tops among the reasons that today's Ozark forests are mostly second and third growth.

The Ozark Mountains are rife with music and lore. Bob McCoy and Lonnie Hoppers, native Ozarkers and master music makers, recalled the ways in which musicians were employed in the Ozarks of the Depression and war eras at dance halls and music parties.

"We played at dance halls and roadhouses," Hoppers said. "For the most part, people came to have a few drinks and dance, but there would be a rough crowd that would show up most of the time, and things could get pretty exciting." Both men recalled that they favored venues with an upright piano on the stage—and it wasn't because they wanted to play it.

"We'd get behind it when the fights started," Hoppers explained.

"There were music parties," McCoy recalled. "People would have them at their house. The musicians would sit in a doorway so that two rooms could be used for dancing."

Hoppers said that these gatherings were much more congenial than those at the dance halls on weekend nights.

"There was never any fighting at the music parties, and the liquor bottles were left outside the house in the woodpile," Hoppers noted. "That was the problem with being in the band; you couldn't go out to the woodpile, you had to sit and play."

Jack Hurst acknowledged the importance of the Ozarks in country music in the front matter of his 1975 book, *Nashville's Grand Ole Opry*. In the attribution of an old witticism, he noted that it was "1920s-vintage wit from the Ozarks, the region and era that inspired the Grand Ole Opry."

Lee and Joyce Mace were born in 1927 and 1925, respectively. In the course of their lifetimes, the Ozark culture of old would alter and fade as modern technology invaded their native hills. It is important to remember that they were born in a time before electricity came to the Ozarks (what radios there were in the mountains of those days were battery powered) and before there were many roads that could

John Vernon Williams and Joyce (Williams) Mace, late 1920s. *Courtesy Joyce Mace.*

accommodate automobiles. It was a life of considerable isolation and not a little hardship. The proud population of the Ozarks had to work hard to make their society work—more so when times were hard everywhere.

Lee once said that many Ozarkers would not accept "relief" during the Depression years. He quoted an "old man" who wouldn't "accept money from the government when relief came." Lee recalled that the old man said, "As long as there are acorns on the trees, I won't accept commodities."

Joyce was the daughter of a relatively prosperous farmer. Her recollections of childhood are happy, but later in life she realized that the family faced Depression-era difficulties that her parents disguised.

"My mother and father pretended to really like the neck and back bone [meat] of chicken," said Joyce. "It wasn't until years later that I realized they did that so we [children] would have the rest to eat."

The Williams family grocery store, 1937. *From left rear*: John T., Audrey and John Vernon. *Front*: Carl and Joyce. Brother Bob refused to pose. *Courtesy Joyce Mace.*

The family's fortunes, though, were solid enough by the late 1930s to enable them to open a grocery store in Osage Beach.

Lee's father, Lucian, was a farmer but also a successful businessman. At one point, he and Tolliver Lawson owned an automobile dealership in Tuscumbia. Lucian Mace was elected sheriff of Miller County. He was later elected to the state legislature. Both of Lee's parents taught school. It is likely that there was more cash-money available to Lee's family than to most Ozarkers of the era. But the Depression years touched everyone who lived through them.

The inherent work ethic of the Ozarks combined with the harsh realities of the Great Depression to create a determined appetite for accomplishment and excellence in the Maces' generation of Ozarkers. In the case of Lee and Joyce Mace, that ethic was applied to another Ozark legacy: music.

The introduction to a mid-1960s Ozark Opry program encapsulated Lee's early musical experience:

Lee's father, Lucian Mace. Lee was proud of his Native American heritage. *Missouri State Archives*.

Lee's mother, Clare Mace. *Photo by Tom Reeves, courtesy Joyce Mace.*

"When I was six," said Lee, "mom set out to make a fiddle player out of me. She liked songs like Row Row Row Your Boat. I liked tunes like Ragtime Annie." By the time he was in second grade, Lee also learned to pick a little on the guitar and high school kids often gave him pennies to play for them. At 13, he learned the unique little jig step that sets Ozark square dancing apart from the western style and within a few years, Lee and some of his friends were good enough to put on square dancing exhibitions at dances and picnics in the Lake of the Ozarks area.

4
LOOSE TAPS

In 1948, Tolliver Lawson, a Miller County millworker and highly regarded practitioner of the Ozark Mountain jig, traveled to Kansas City for a somewhat extended visit, probably staying with one of his sisters who lived there.

As if to prove the characterization of Missouri as the place where the "Old South meets the New West," Tolliver went to a western-style square dance while living in the city. He watched the proceedings with interest. The movement and footwork of each dancer were exactly the same, and all of the "sets" (groups of dancers) moved to the instruction of one caller.

Whereas the purpose of the western-style square dance was group expression, the Ozark Mountain jig was about individual expression. A caller may instruct the general movement of jig dancers in a common direction, but the footwork and body movement are unique to each individual dancer's desires. Each set of dancers usually has its own caller, and the dancers follow the music as much as they do the calls.

What caught young Tolliver's attention, however, was not the uniform choreography or the different method of calling the dance but the fact that the dancers had metal "tap" plates affixed to the soles of their shoes. The effect of actually hearing the dance steps was, to the young jig dancer from the Ozarks, electrifying. The trick, he was told, was to put the taps on "loose" to achieve a castanets-like sound effect.

Tolliver Lawson returned home to Tuscumbia with loose taps on the soles of his dancing shoes, and he astounded all his friends at the next dance. "I had seen tap dancers in the movies," Lee Mace would tell an interviewer decades later, "but we had never thought of putting taps on to jig."

Following Tolliver's lead, Lee and the other jig dancers got taps of their own, and, Lee related, they "tore up the Tuscumbia Picnic" that year and would soon tear up venues across the nation.

Sarah Gertrude Knott founded the National Folk Festival in 1934. After the inaugural "National," as it has come to be known, in St. Louis, the festival began the touring from city to city that has become its hallmark.

In 1938, Eleanor Roosevelt accepted the honorary chair of the festival, and the show moved to Washington, D.C., for five years.

The National returned to St. Louis for an extended run from 1947 to 1955. Since then, it has moved fairly frequently to cities around the country. Its relocations can be tracked on the Internet.

The National is the grand dame of American folk music festivals and is vigorously inclusive of all sort of folk music.

In 1948, Knott contacted the Camdenton Chamber of Commerce, inquiring about music and dance performers representative of Ozark culture. It is highly probable that someone immediately thought of Lee, Joyce, Carl, Tolliver and their tap-shod, jig-dancing troupe that had "torn up" the Tuscumbia Picnic. The group dubbed themselves the "Lake of the Ozarks Square Dancers" and performed in the 1948 National at Kiel Opera House in St. Louis.

The Lake of the Ozarks Square Dancers' personnel varied; the first caller was Glenn Morgan, and his two daughters were in the mix of dancers. But the troupe that would soon travel the nation consisted of Lee and Joyce Mace; Tolliver Lawson and his niece, Kathleen Doherty; Carl Williams and his wife, Eileen; Dillard Stamper; and Nellie Abbott.

Billie Morris provided musical accompaniment on tenor banjo, Gene Spencer on guitar and Jim Skiles on fiddle. Spurgeon Atwell was the caller. Jim Skiles and Nellie Abbott would later marry.

The performance at Kiel was a triumph. The Lake of the Ozark Square Dancers was in demand throughout the Ozarks and beyond. The troupe played the 1950 Chicago Fair, sponsored by Lake of the Ozarks merchants and the Camdenton Chamber of Commerce. It made a similar trip to the Kansas City centennial that year.

The troupe also participated in exhibitions throughout the Ozarks. Joyce Mace recollected inadvertently winning a jig contest at a turkey-calling contest in Eureka Springs, Arkansas, in 1949. Under the impression that the event was an exhibition, she danced as long as the music played. She thought it a bit strange that dancers were being tapped on the shoulder and escorted from the dance floor, but she continued to dance until only a few

Lee (center) and Joyce Mace at the Palais Club with unidentified jig dancers. Jim and Mary von Gremp are in the background (left). *Courtesy Joyce Mace.*

The Lake of the Ozark Square Dancers at the Chicago Fair, 1950. Carl Williams and Joyce Mace are in the foreground. Catherine Morgan is behind Joyce. Note the logo on the shirt and skirts. *Courtesy Joyce Mace.*

remained, and then Joyce was declared the winner. The prize was a pair of tiny wooden jig dancers on a platform, with facial features impressed on what appear to be small tree nuts. Joyce has kept it in her possession ever since.

Lee Mace received an army draft notice shortly after he and Joyce married in 1950. He had served one year of active duty with the navy at the end of

The jig dance trophy, Eureka Springs, Arkansas, late 1940s. *Courtesy Joyce Mace.*

World War II, even taking early graduation from high school to do so. And Lee had been in the U.S. Naval Reserve for four years after active duty. He had fulfilled completely any obligation for military service. Nonetheless, in 1950, he was drafted into the army during the Korean War.

"They told him he shouldn't be drafted right up to the day that he was inducted," Joyce said.

Lee served his country for two more years without complaint. And, as always, he came away with a positive experience. He had learned to play the bass fiddle in the slap-happy style that would become an integral part of his personal signature.

While stationed in France, Lee and some fellow GIs formed a band. It was decided that they needed a bass to round out their sound. In what was certainly a remarkable coincidence, they soon found one—in a dump. From whence it came was never determined.

The salvaged bass had a broken neck. Lee's army buddy and lifelong friend Jim Logue, from Stafford, Kansas, had a solution. He took a baseball bat and, with the use of a lathe, sanded and shaped it to match the neck of the bass. A little glue and nail, and voila! Lee had a bass fiddle to play. He brought it back to the United States with him, and it was the instrument he played for many years. It sits today in the living room of the house that he and Joyce built in 1957.

While Lee was away, Joyce was busy preparing for his return. She found work as a waitress at the Kirkwood Lodge resort in Osage Beach. In an interesting connection, Kirkwood Lodge would become a mecca of the

Lee Mace with his baseball bat bass, 1953. *Courtesy Joyce Mace.*

square dance world. To this day, people take square dance vacations at Kirkwood Lodge, with classes and workshops during the day and dancing at night.

Joyce made good tips at Kirkwood Lodge and saved up enough money to buy a little house in Linn Creek. The house had been moved from Old Linn Creek when Bagnell Dam was completed and the waters that formed the Lake of the Ozarks flooded the original town.

To prepare for the flood, much of Old Linn Creek had simply been torched, burned to the ground. But a few residents would not part with their homes and had picked them up and moved them to higher ground. Joyce bought one of those relocated houses in 1951 for $2,500.

"Imagine moving a house in those days," Joyce said. At that time, probably 1930, the move would almost certainly have been accomplished with manual labor and mule teams over some rough and rocky roads. But that house was, after all, someone's home and therefore worth the effort.

5

THE LAKE, LEE AND CYRUS CRANE WILLMORE

The great utility and public works projects of the Depression era have left an indelible notch in the American collective unconscious. The legacy of those works that lives on in the national memory is the awareness that the creation of the Lake of the Ozarks and similar projects meant the destruction of farms and homes, the moving of cemeteries and buildings and the displacement of families from land they may have lived on for generations.

But the clearing of land and the dam construction were an enormous boon to the area. The work went on day and night, and thousands were employed for cash-money wages. According to Doc Foster, the pay for a laborer was thirty-five or forty cents an hour, and there was a mess hall where hearty food was plentiful.

"I attended the dedication of the dam in 1931 with my parents," Lee once recalled for a reporter. "A lot of the old-timers said the lake would never fill, but we had an unusually wet year and it filled a year and a half ahead of schedule." The lake began filling on February 2, 1931, and reached "spillway crest elevation" on May 20, 1931.

Some residents of the Three County area (Morgan, Miller and Camden) who were most affected by the construction of Bagnell Dam felt that even if the reservoir area filled with water, the dam itself would not hold.

In an account of the construction of Bagnell Dam dated January 16, 1931, the *Versailles Leader* newspaper printed an article that appears to be an attempt to reassure the public of the safety and soundness of the soon-to-be-operational dam:

Within a few miles of Versailles an epic battle is in progress with the forces of nature opposed to the skill and science of man. Here a mighty river is being subdued and made to work for civilization. However, the completion of the great dam in April, the closing of the gates and the gradual filling of the 60,000 acre Lake of the Ozarks does not mark the complete defeat of the great Osage River.

Skilled engineers have considered it a worthy foe and have taken all precaution against its strength, knowing that it will be continually at work throughout the years to undermine the dam which obstructs its natural course, and while it will be harnessed and controlled it will retain its strength.

The first step in guarding against the pressure of the water was taken when the bed rock, on which the concrete structure rests, was made practically water tight by forcing concrete by compressed air into numerous holes drilled in the rock. Under this pressure the concrete spread though-out all minute crevices and fissures in the rock, preventing water collecting in these spaces until the dam was finally undermined. When the concrete of the main dam was poured upon this reinforced base it united with it as single mass. The rock bluffs at each end of the one half mile dam were treated in the same manner.

Seepage was taken care of from this source but care was also taken to prevent water seeping through the solid concrete body of the dam, for with the terrific pressure against it solid concrete could not remain impervious to the water. So below the high water line a length of sheet copper, one-sixteenth of an inch thick and 100 feet wide, was embedded in the concrete along the whole upper face of the dam. To catch the water, which under pressure would penetrate this metal, rows of iron pipes punched full of holes were placed vertically the length of the dam, so that seepage would collect in these and be led downward to the base where it would drain off below the dam itself.

Another safeguard which testifies to the elaborate care and consideration for safety which imbues these engineers is the construction of a tunnel through the dam from end to end. This is large enough for a man to walk through, and after the completion of the dam a watchman will patrol this passage, watching for signs of seepage out of the concrete, for the mighty Osage will work unceasingly.

The reported sixteenth of an inch copper sheet probably did not convey as much comfort as was intended. Certainly the article might have better accomplished its purpose had there been fewer references to the might and

An aerial view of Bagnell Dam and lake. *Missouri State Archives.*

determination of the Osage River. It could be said that the Osage River was dammed with faint praise.

The local wisdom is that the lake did not become a tourist destination until the late 1940s because of the Great Depression and World War II. Certainly those events were major influences on the way people used their time and money.

But Union Electric (UE), the builder and owner of Bagnell Dam and the entire shoreline it created, did little to facilitate development of the lake until 1945.

UE (now AmerenUE) sold the lake's shoreline to the Willmore Company for $320,000. All told, this included forty thousand acres of lakefront property with eight hundred miles of shoreline, a hotel the utility had built, cottages, pleasure boats, the Adirondack-style "great camp" building and the soon rechristened Willmore Lodge, named for the man who benefited from the transaction, Cyrus Crane Willmore.

Willmore converted the structure, originally a place to entertain important guests and executives of UE, into his personal residence.

Al Elam was a prominent Ozarker whose career as an engineer, surveyor and real estate investor and broker was entwined with the construction of Bagnell Dam and the development of the Lake of the Ozarks as a property. In a private recorded interview, he described the crux of the transaction and Willmore:

> *Union Electric had to sell the shoreline because in 1945 the SEC ordered them and all public utilities to divest any business not related to utilities.*
>
> *Cy really wanted to be a country squire. He wanted to keep Horseshoe Bend and Shawnee Bend and sell the rest.*

In 1945, $320,000 was a great deal of money, but the value of what was sold—the lakefront acreage and shoreline of a fifty-four-thousand-acre commercially exploitable lake—is staggering in comparison to what Willmore paid for it.

Like another aspiring country gentleman, Ha Ha Tonka's Robert Snyder, Willmore—a charismatic, larger-than-life figure—had little time to enjoy his Ozark estate. He died of heart disease in 1949. In his obituary in the *St. Louis Globe-Democrat* on April 11, 1949, he was described as "the last of the old time real estate promoters."

Cyrus Willmore (seated) entertains at the lake, 1947. *Missouri State Archives.*

A public document, the "National Register of Historic Places Registration Form—Willmore Lodge," was prepared and filed for AmerenUE in 1998 by Laura Johnson, preservationist, with Benjamin Cawthra, historian, for the purpose of achieving the designation of Willmore Lodge as a Historic Place.

The document tells a somewhat more complete story of Willmore's acquisition of the shoreline and lodge than did Al Elam. The lodge was initially known as Egan's Lodge, named for the UE president, Louis Egan:

> *Egan facilitated the good times by building a boat dock at the water's edge accessed by an elaborate tram system that transported guests from the lodge down to the lake. Lodge guests had twenty-five duck blinds from which to choose, accessed by roads built to points along Horseshoe Bend, the first roads built on the peninsula.*
>
> *Egan's Lodge was far more than an innocent retreat for company executives, however, and the building played a prominent role in the scandal that led to its eventual sale in 1945. As Union Electric pushed for greater coverage of the region's power needs following the completion of the dam in the 1930s, its interests often clashed with those of local residents who favored alternatives to the powerful company in the form of municipally generated and owned power.*

The upshot was that UE, in an attempt to monopolize the distribution of electricity in the region, began to engage in illegal lobbying activities, many of which involved entertaining at the lodge. The Securities and Exchange Commission got involved, and by mid-1939 all the top executives at UE had resigned. The lodge was put up for sale in 1941 with no takers until Cyrus Crane Willmore happened upon the scene.

The National Registry form lists the following contribution Willmore made to the development of the Lake of the Ozarks as a recreation destination:

> *Willmore created the Lake of the Ozarks Lodge properties, and made plans for development of the land. In the first couple of years after his purchase of the Union Electric property, he created twenty-five miles of road on his property and began selling to other developers. In 1946, he initiated speedboat races on the lake to generate interest in the area's recreational possibilities.*

In 1947, Willmore hired Lee Mace and Ernest McNeil to build the twenty-five miles of road he needed to access his property at the dam. Joyce recalls that Lee said he had greatly enjoyed the job—it often involved operating a bulldozer, which a young Lee Mace would have loved doing.

Ernest McNeil related that Willmore often toured the property in a pickup, talking about a wide range of subjects, in particular his plans for the lake. It is very likely that Lee put to use later in life much of what he learned from this experience. A recurring pattern in Lee's younger life was his personal contact with legendary promoters, developers, artists and entrepreneurs, experiences from which he gained valuable knowledge.

The marketing efforts of the Willmore Company and the developers with whom Cyrus Willmore did business in the Lake of the Ozarks deal, Al Elam and others, changed the cultural climate of the northern Ozarks considerably.

When Lee Mace returned from the army in 1952, he found a steady flow of tourist traffic that was beginning to support business expansion. Tourist courts or camps, the forerunners of the motel industry, were adding cabins and building restaurant additions onto their offices. Water-skiing was becoming popular. There was more than just hunting and fishing going on, and Lee, no doubt, saw great opportunity in that fact.

6
1953

In 1953, Ted Mack and *The Original Amateur Hour* came to Kansas City to hold auditions. *The Original Amateur Hour* is an American icon and to this day maintains an Internet presence. The website originalamateurhour.com describes the show:

> *Long before TV's* American Idol *became a mega-hit, there was one radio and television series that started the talent competition craze. It was called:* The Original Amateur Hour. *On TV the host was Ted Mack. On radio it was Major Edward Bowes and on cable it was Willard Scott. Almost 50 major stars of movies, records, stage, screen and television got their start on this series. This is the show that made the "gong" famous as well as "the wheel of fortune" and the phrase: "'round and 'round she goes, and where she stops, nobody knows."*

Lee and Joyce Mace and the Ozark jig ensemble traveled to Kansas City to test their fortune with Ted Mack. Out of seventeen hundred auditions, four performers were chosen to appear on the nationally broadcast show. One of those acts was the Lake of the Ozarks Square Dancers. The troupe appeared twice on *The Original Amateur Hour*, first in Kansas City on June 13, 1953, and next at the show's New York studios on the Fourth of July. "We went to New York by train," Joyce remembered. "It was the first time I had ever been on a train—I think it was the first time most of us had."

After seeing the group on *The Original Amateur Hour*, the Grand Ole Opry hired it to perform with the show at Ryman Auditorium. It was the first time tap-shod square dancers, later a staple, would appear on the Grand Ole

Opry stage. The only condition was a name change to the Grand Ole Opry Square Dancers. The Ozark jig dancers readily agreed.

As part of the deal, the Lake of the Ozarks/Grand Ole Opry Square Dancers, along with Lee and Joyce, were also to perform at the 1953 WSM Disk Jockey (DJ) Festival.

The year 1953 is generally considered to be "Year One" in the history of the modern country music industry. It is significant that that same year marked the founding of the Ozark Opry, an entertainment concept that was the model for the industry's alternative dimension, now known as Branson-style venues.

At Hank Williams's funeral on January 4, 1953, more than twenty thousand people came to pay their respects. For a "hillbilly" musician to receive that much attention in those days shocked and awed the entire American music industry and media.

The Hank Williams phenomenon could not have come at a better time for those who were trying to move country music into the mainstream of the entertainment industry, namely Nashville stars Ernest Tubb, Hank Snow and Roy Acuff, among others.

Tubb is said to be the man who persuaded Decca Records to change its catalogue heading from "Hill Billy" to "Country and Western." He also successfully talked the Grand Ole Opry announcers into dropping the word hillbilly from their patter.

It is important to note that the stakes for country music performers and composers of that time were very high. The organizations BMI and ASCAP, which collected performance fees or royalties for the music industry, had been slow in acknowledging the hillbilly market. This meant that the royalty agencies did not always monitor performances or enforce normal payment procedures for the hillbilly composers and performers. The same thing was true for the "race" record industry. As far as the American music industry was concerned, these genres were too eccentric to try to service. That is what Tubb and his Nashville allies desperately needed to change. And they would succeed.

Hank Snow and Ernest Tubb were instrumental in the next major occurrence in country music that year. In May 1953, the pair staged a concert and dedication of a memorial to country music artist Jimmie Rodgers. (Tubb was absent from the festivities, according to Ronnie Pugh's biography, due to a bout with the bottle.) The event, "Jimmie Rodgers Memorial Day," took place in the town of Rodgers's birth: Meridian, Mississippi.

Snow and Tubb paid tribute to the man whom Tubb called the "Daddy of Country Music." Snow named one of his son's Jimmie Rodgers Snow, and Tubb had assumed something of Rodgers's patriarchal musical mantle, playing and posing often with a "$1,500 guitar" that had belonged to Rodgers.

The event was considered a success, with upwards of twenty-five thousand fans of Rodgers and country music in attendance.

But it was the 1953 WSM DJ Festival that really caught the attention of the mainstream music industry. This was the second annual such festival, and the fledgling Nashville establishment had "bet the farm" on it. Nothing was spared in getting maximum attendance and media coverage.

The media was there. Dave Garroway brought the *Today* show from New York, and among his guests were the Grand Ole Opry Square Dancers, Lee and Joyce Mace and the jig troupe. *Today* was the second national television show they appeared on that year.

Upwards of six hundred attendees were reported to have been at the DJ festival, the majority of whom were DJs from all across the country. There were hospitality suites and receptions hosted by major record labels. The president of BMI, a major music rights licensing organization, was present and promised support to the country music industry.

Billboard ran a slightly breathless article on the festival in its November 28, 1953 issue: "WSM's DJ Festival Public Relations Coup."

Country music, and Nashville, had arrived as an industry. One question that remained, phrased in the language of the dawning electronic age: was country music ready for prime time?

One of the major cultural changes of the post–World War II era was the advent of television. The new medium created a demand for visual content. The jig dance rhythms and flashing footwork of the Grand Ole Opry Square Dancers (aka Lake of the Ozarks Square Dancers) were just the things to jumpstart country music television.

7

LEE, SEYMOUR WEISS
AND AL GANNAWAY

The Ted Mack appearance brought Lee and Joyce Mace and the Lake of the Ozarks Square Dancers to the attention of New Orleans promoter and hotel owner Seymour Weiss. Weiss is remembered today as the treasurer for and confidante of—some even say the power behind—Huey P. Long Jr. Weiss served sixteen months in prison for tax evasion and mail fraud in the early 1940s but received a full and unconditional pardon from President Harry Truman in 1947.

Seymour Weiss was, above all, a master promoter and entrepreneur who had established his palatial Roosevelt Hotel as the "Pride of the South" and its Blue Room, which was blue indeed with stars painted on the ceiling, as the venue for top name entertainment in New Orleans. Informants said that Weiss had called the Ted Mack show immediately after seeing the Ozarkers perform and booked them on the spot. Mack announced it on the show.

The Ozark jig dancers were booked for a month in the Blue Room, where they appeared under their original name, the Lake of the Ozarks Square Dancers. They were the opening act for Chuck Foster's orchestra.

The Chuck Foster orchestra was a popular big band that had been playing major venues since the 1930s. The big band era was still strong in the 1950s, and the Foster band was a major draw. Its eponymous founder, Chuck Foster, was a popular movie-idol, handsome bandleader and singer. The band's theme song was "Oh! You Beautiful Doll!" Foster would single out a woman in the audience during each show and sing directly to her.

But after the first night's performance, Seymour Weiss moved the Lake of the Ozarks Square Dancers to the top of the bill.

The Lake of the Ozarks Square Dancers with Chuck Foster (center) at the Blue Room. On the left are Bill and Betty Hagedorn, owners of Kirkwood Lodge, who drove to New Orleans to see the show. *Courtesy Joyce Mace.*

"It was so exciting," Joyce Mace recalled, "when we saw the marquee the next morning and we had been put at the top."

Seymour Weiss was well aware of his celebrity status, as evidenced by the fact that he autographed Lee and Joyce Mace's souvenir program in flourished script with an old-fashioned spiraled ampersand: "To Mr. & Mrs. Lee Mace with my kindest regards and best wishes. Sincerely."

Following the Blue Room engagement, the Ozark jig-dancing troupe did a month at another famous venue, the Riverside Hotel in Reno, said to be built on the exact spot where the City of Reno was founded and owned for much of its history by another controversial entrepreneur, George Wingfield.

The Lake of the Ozarks Square Dancers was top billed in Reno. The advertisement copy tells it all: "Real Old Fashioned 'Hoe Downs' to the tune of the six piece Hill-Billy Symphony! Something entirely new in entertainment!"

There was also a weekend engagement in Las Vegas, although no one recalled the exact name of the venue.

From 1954 to 1956, Lee, Joyce and their Ozark jig troupe, performing as the Grand Ole Opry Square Dancers, filmed about one hundred television shows with the Grand Ole Opry. Among other firsts in their careers, Lee and Joyce were on the stage for the first television broadcasts of *The Grand Ole Opry*.

WSM–Grand Ole Opry had established WSM-TV in 1950. It was Nashville's only television station for several years. But even so, the Grand Ole Opry and

The Lake of the Ozarks Square Dancers' billing at the Riverside in Reno. *Courtesy Joyce Mace.*

its corporate owner, doing more reckoning than reasoning, had been slow to move into television, fearing that doing so would dilute the hegemony the show had established in the radio market.

As the WSM–Grand Ole Opry management and their bosses struggled to understand the new medium, others were getting into television with enthusiasm.

Over in the Ozarks in Springfield, Missouri, Red Foley and top Nashville talent manager Dub Albritten were putting together a deal that would lead to the first national network country music show to feature top country stars as guest artists: *Ozark Jubilee*.

Ozark Jubilee premiered its live stage show on January 22, 1955, beating the Grand Ole Opry to national television by nearly a year, and even then the opry initially broadcast only a slight portion of its radio stage show.

However, WSM–Grand Ole Opry did begin broadcasting and distributing a thirty-minute filmed show, *The Country Show: With Stars of the Grand Ole Opry*, the week of January 20, 1955, the same week *Ozark Jubilee* went national.

WSM had signed a contract with producer Albert C. Gannaway, Jr. and Flamingo Films to film shows for television for the next five years, sealing the deal on August 18, 1954.

Production of *The Country Show* commenced in November 1954 and ceased in December 1956, when Gannaway's backers ran out of credit. The twenty-two-minute films were shot in a series of grueling six-day workweeks. The filming was done in a Quonset hut in which a barn and barnyard set had been constructed. Joyce Mace remembered that it was called "the old barn."

Much to the chagrin of the WSM–Grand Ole Opry honchos, *The Country Show* was to become a treasure-trove for Gannaway, who held exclusive reissue rights; in those days, it had not occurred to many that such rights might have value. That Gannaway filmed the shows in color enhanced that value considerably.

In the years to come, WSM attempted but was unsuccessful in getting the courts to set aside Gannaway's contract.

What was often overlooked but was discussed in detail in the November 28, 1953 *Billboard* article was that WSM–Grand Ole Opry was a wholly owned subsidiary of the National Life & Accident Company. "Much of its [the insurance company's] success is attributed to the good will created by the 'Grand Ole Opry' program and its talent," *Billboard* noted.

But the WSM–Grand Ole Opry executives would, in the space of a couple of years, be out to do more than sell insurance. They would be in a better position to act under their own power than had been generally realized to that point.

The first stirrings of a move to own or control anything having to do with the new country and western music industry were underway. The Nashville establishment that was coming into being in the 1950s would very successfully do just that.

Albert Gannaway's trump of WSM's hand was an exception to the rule. There would be a few others—early country music "outlaws"—who went their own way and prospered, as did Lee and Joyce Mace. But for the most part, WSM and its affiliates would control the new country music industry.

The Gannaway films are on the market to this day in their entirety at various websites, notably countrymusictreasures.com. There are twelve ninety-four-minute color DVDs titled *Memories: Country Music Stars of the Fifties—The Al Gannaway Collection.* In the online Country Music Treasures promotional notes, Lee and Joyce Mace et al are referred to as the "Original Grand Ole Opry Square Dancers."

Over a half century after the filming, the Ozark Mountain jig-dancing friends who became stars of the Grand Ole Opry are still dancing their tap-shod jigs on video and no doubt will be doing so far into the future. And it is likely that when Ozark-style dancing is depicted in films—as it was in *O Brother, Where Art Thou?*, the 2000 Coen brothers film—it was somewhere along the way inspired or informed by the dancing on the Gannaway shows.

Of interest is the fact that Lee and Joyce and their fellow jig dancers got as much or more airtime in the Gannaway films than most of the guest artists. They opened the show, did a number in the middle and closed the show. The hosts and guest artists danced with them. A very memorable segment shows "Little" Jimmy Dickens riding the back of Lee's bass fiddle as Lee circles the dancers. The unique talent and preparation of the group of jig dancers from the Ozarks had met with perfect opportunity. It all seemed ready made and effortless.

But Lee and Joyce were not just showing up for work; they were observing and learning from some of the most accomplished performers and entrepreneurs in the entertainment industry and making conscious business choices. Carl Williams summed it up for a reporter in 1985: "Lee had the ability to watch everything and remember."

Now pause the narrative and consider what had occurred. Lee and Joyce Mace and the Lake of the Ozark Square Dancers had effortlessly accomplished what, in spite of a determined Herculean effort, the country music industry had not. They had appeared to great acclaim on national television. They had played major entertainment venues to even more acclaim (immediately bumped to top billing over popular acts). The hillbilly dancers and their "Hilly-Billy Symphony" had made it in show business—mainstream show business, playing to urban audiences—which was exactly what Tubb, Snow, Acuff and their cohort so desperately desired. No wonder WSM immediately sought to bring the dancers into the fold.

Lee and Joyce had made it in Nashville. They were the "Original Grand Ole Opry Square Dancers." The troupe had offers and endorsements (Lee Jeans). The Ozarkers were the toast of the town. The Maces could have moved to Nashville and made a good living in the new country music industry. But they had another plan.

Joyce Mace's fondest memory of the Gannaway filming is the times that Mother Maybelle Carter invited the Ozarkers to her house for dinner and rounds of poker.

"Lee loved to play poker," Joyce said. "And so did Mother Maybelle; she kept her poker money in a little pouch and was always ready to play."

8

THE HILLBILLY AS
PERFORMANCE ART

In addition to the run on national television, the Roosevelt Hotel, the Reno and Vegas shows, the 1953 WSM DJ Festival and the Gannaway filming, Lee was hired as program director and DJ at KRMS radio back at the Lake of the Ozarks.

Robert M. Smith, the owner whose initials were the call letters of the station, had imported experienced radio operators from Kansas City and was the station's initial program director. Therein lay a problem: few Ozarkers would listen to the brand of popular music the city folk favored. KRMS had few listeners and thus few advertisers.

Robert M. Smith and his station manager, James Ellis ("Jim") von Gremp, hired the young Lee Mace, now a nationally recognized artist and a locally lionized expert on the music of the region, as program director and DJ.

The first thing Lee did was to quash the city music. The next move Lee made was to open the radio studio every Sunday afternoon to anyone who wanted to come in and play or sing. This was the genesis of the talent show and auditions that he would host at the Ozark Opry for the rest of his life.

The station quickly began featuring a crew of studio musicians playing traditional Ozark music. This group would become the Ozark Opry.

The practice of radio stations employing live musicians had been necessary in the early days of radio and was still a fairly common practice in the late 1940s into the 1950s.

Decades later, an article was published in the Hermitage, Missouri newspaper *Index* about members of the first Ozark Opry cast—Lonnie Hoppers, Bob Penny and Bob McCoy:

As the decade of the fifties was beginning, the three and an Urbana fiddle player named Orvil Day decided to enter the weekly talent contest being sponsored by KRMS radio in Osage Beach, Mo. When radio station manager Jim von Gremp heard them perform, he hired them to be the stage band for the weekly contests so contestants could have an accompaniment band.

"We went there hoping to enter the contest," Hoppers recalls, "and ended up not getting to compete because we were hired by the radio station."

"Performing on the radio was considered hitting the big time in those days," Hoppers says. And the group was excited about performing on the air and performing for the weekly contests.

That's when the group met the man who would single-handedly direct their musical careers and impact Ozarks music more than any other individual. Lee Mace, a disk jockey on KRMS radio, was the master of ceremonies for the radio station's talent contests, and joined the group playing the bass fiddle.

Ozark Opry, 1953. Jim von Gremp and his son (also Jim) are in the foreground. *From left*: Bob "High Pockets" McCoy, Ramona Bullington, Lee, Basil Robinette, Lonnie Hoppers, Annie Rambo, "Bashful Bob" Penny and Billie Moore. *Courtesy Joyce Mace.*

Lee had some other ideas for promotion of the station. Smith and Jim von Gremp were more than happy to go along with whatever their newly found DJ and consultant came up with.

One of those ideas was to sponsor live music shows, featuring hillbilly performers, on the tourist strip of trinket shops, cafés and saloons that had taken root next to Bagnell Dam. There was a building there known as the Casino, which housed a café and gift shop. Today, the building is historic, the first structure to be erected on the West End of Bagnell Dam. Union Electric built the Lakeside Casino Restaurant to "serve visitors to the lake and the dam." The lower levels of the building opened out onto a view of the lake and dam. Lee, von Gremp and Smith reckoned they could squeeze a couple hundred folding chairs into the small space, take the microphone and amplifiers from the radio station and put on a show for the tourists, who would then tune in to KRMS, generating advertising sales from the rapidly growing number of area businesses catering to the tourist trade.

> *"Lee made it work with his enthusiasm and promotional abilities,"* Hoppers said. *"He dressed us up like hillbillies and made the Highpockets character for Bob McCoy and the Bashful Bob character for Bob Penny. And the people seemed to love it."*

The West End of Bagnell Dam, mid-1950s. The Lakeside Casino Restaurant is visible at left. *Missouri State Archives.*

The Hillbilly as Performance Art

As to the hillbilly aspect of the show, Lee Mace told a reporter decades later, "Folks were coming from Chicago and the first thing they wanted to see was the Dam, the next thing was a hillbilly. Well, we figured we would show them a hillbilly even if we had to go to Chicago and hire one."

The term "hillbilly" is said to have been coined by a country musician of the 1920s, Al Hopkins, who named his band The Hill Billies. Although some academics have tried to complicate the matter, it seems a straightforward assumption that the word is a combination of "hill" and the common designation of an animal associated with hilly topography, a billy goat.

The term came to be associated with the kind of music Hopkins made—early country music—and bands that played in that style. Then the word hillbilly was attached to general rural culture, usually as a pejorative.

What is most telling in the understanding of the Ozark Opry as it positioned itself in the emerging country music industry is that Lee Mace embraced the term hillbilly. Through a marketing lens, the separate strategies of Nashville and Lee Mace become crystal clear. Lee saw that by positioning hillbilly music and dance as an exciting "new kind of entertainment," he could win audiences otherwise not accessible.

In contrast, a voice from Nashville in the early 1950s might have proclaimed: "Ain't no hillbillies here. Call us country—practically suburbanites. Our music is like pop music. Almost the same." This positioning, it was hoped, would win audiences for the newly minted country and western music.

Lee was selling "different"; Nashville was selling "same." Both would succeed.

Thus was the Ozark Opry founded in 1953 at the conceptual polar opposite of the conventional wisdom and wishes of the emergent country music industry—and it would remain so for the entire course of events.

Meanwhile, back at the lake. With the masterful connectivity of vision that would characterize his entire business career, Lee saw how drawing tourists in to witness a hillbilly music show by real hillbillies would create interest in tuning in to the radio station KRMS to listen to a real hillbilly show of the same name, *The Ozark Opry*.

The overall package was presented to the city folk as a musical novelty. Because, put simply, even though the Nashville establishment was agitating to create a category called country and western in the corporate and cultural music catalogue, it had not arrived at that destination in 1953. Most of the city folk visiting the Lake of the Ozarks had not heard much, if any, of the country music genre.

Lee already had the locals listening faithfully to **KRMS**; if he could expand the radio station's audience to the tourists, whose numbers were increasing each year, he might be able to shoot the moon.

So he put *The Ozark Opry* cast, all excellent country musicians, in rustic clothing and set to work. Although some early country music performers had dressed in rural work garb, their audiences were generally rural. But *The Ozark Opry* stage show had something that the country music shows of the time did not: entertainment based on back story, a performance art type of show with a non-narrative thread spun from the popular perception of hillbilly culture that gave context to the music and comedy of the show.

The Ozark Opry concept also contained the expectation of a different kind of audience than most previous country music performers had presumed. Even the urban-based *Barn Dance* radio shows were directed toward a rural audience, either through clear channel broadcasting to rural areas or to audiences of rural migrants to the cities.

Quite to the contrary, the Ozark Opry's premise presumed an urban audience.

Ozark Opry, 1956. *From left*: Lonnie Hoppers, Art Reed, Don Russell, "Bashful Bob," Faith Fowler, "High Pockets," Lee and Dillard Stamper. *Courtesy Helen Russell.*

The early *Opry* cast was dressed in what city folk might think of as typical hillbilly costumes. *The Ozark Opry* show was a loose montage presenting a collection of good-natured hillbillies putting on entertainment for visitors from the city.

Lee was careful in early radio shows to give notice that although the music of the show was "country, we put on a good show." He noted also that tickets were ninety cents (thirty-five cents for children). In those days, the show started at 9:00 p.m. because, Joyce Mace recalled, "people were on the lake until then."

Darrel Gordon, who was a guitar player and lead singer with the Ozark Opry from 1963 to 1965—toward the end of the hillbilly days—attested to the success of Lee's initial back story:

> *People in the audience, mostly from cities like Chicago, would actually ask us* [the performers] *if they could come by the next day and take us in their cars to see "where we really lived." They thought they would see a tar paper shack, a hound dog and moonshine still—they really believed it.*

What was truly unique about *The Ozark Opry* though, was the fact that early on it began to run multiple nights weekly during the tourist season, and the content of the show did not vary greatly from performance to performance. It would soon become the first music show in the country to run six nights a week.

This was a bold new format. The business model was manifold but clear: location, a recreational body of water (the dam) and some attractions, like Indian Burial Cave, to draw tourists; concept, family-oriented performance art (that is, hillbilly with tradition-based music, including some country gospel and a dose of patriotic material); cast, a competent but "starless" ensemble; and audience, families on vacation, tourists, guests and affinity groups from area resorts and residents of the region.

9

THE MONROE STANDARD

The country music situation post 1953 and the events of that year convinced the American music entertainment industry that there was potential in the country music market. The large turnouts for the Williams funeral and the Jimmie Rodgers Memorial Day were of great interest to the industry, and the boffo reaction of the media to the WSM DJ Festival later in the year put many doubts to rest.

There remained unease about the newly dubbed country and western music. The general sense was that country music fans were extraordinarily loyal to the artists and a larger market than previously thought existed. But country music was still too alien and regional to be afforded access to the mainstream music industry's financial and promotion organs. Well into the 1950s, in some reports of the music industry media, the terms "rustic" and "hillbilly" were used to describe that industry segment.

And in the 1950s, what the managers of the emerging country music industry and its image wanted to achieve more than anything else was to convince the rest of the music industry that their segment was as predictable and malleable as any popular genre. What was to be jettisoned in the process of joining the mainstream was a great deal of the respect for the traditional, unshakable loyalty and complete surrender of faith, love and support that country audiences had always rendered to their artists, along with the very idea that any hillbillies were involved in the industry.

Lee Mace did not buy into this new movement. Lee built his career and the success of the Ozark Opry on adherence to the old traditions and values of country music. His respect for the traditional approach to country music and his steadfast faith in the loyalty of audiences is well known.

Lee Mace and "High Pockets" at the Missouri State Fair, mid-1950s. *Missouri State Archives.*

The primary models for country shows in the era of the Ozark Opry's founding were touring troupes, like Bill Monroe's or *Barn Dance* radio shows. Although the precursors of the modern Nashville "package" touring shows had been around since the late 1930s, Monroe was, during much of his career, an independent operator who did not rely on sponsors, promoters, opening acts or guest artists. He was the show, and the show was seldom off the road for long.

In the early days, Monroe sometimes employed a cadre of "advance men" who traveled ahead of the band bus to book venues, publicize coming shows and sell tickets. Then, when the band arrived, the musicians would play a game of baseball with the locals.

Sometimes Monroe would bring his horse, King Wilkie, and, outfitted in riding gear and boots, ride magnificently through the streets of the town. Taken as a whole, the Monroe model created a connection with the audience that few entertainment enterprises could match. In some small towns, a Bill Monroe visitation and performance is recalled with admiration to this day.

Lee Mace brought some of the same magic to venues with his twin engine, four-passenger Aztec airplane. Rural audiences would sometimes follow him to the local airstrip to see the plane take off. And while Lee and the Ozark

Lee Mace with his first airplane. *Courtesy Joyce Mace.*

Opry troupe were never known to play a game of baseball while touring, there was an echo of Monroe's marketing in Lee's invitation to audiences on tour: "We came to see you, now you all come to see us!"

By the 1940s, promoters like Ernest Tubb and Hank Snow were working hard to develop a new country music paradigm. The new model involved touring, but it would most often be seasonal packaged tours, consisting of two to four or more acts and sold from corporate offices to venues across the nation and marketed, managed and promoted from those same offices. Large air-conditioned buses shielded the talent from contact with the public, and such contact was carefully managed.

The new corporate approach to country music directed the audience toward a generic image and sound and a constant diet of new "country pop" tunes rather than individual performers and tradition-based repertoire. By the late 1970s and early 1980s, country record labels were dropping old school country artists en masse in favor of the new generic approach to the market.

In the last quarter of the twentieth century, this approach led a number of country music stars, Willie Nelson and others, to declare that they were "outlaws." At first, the term meant mostly a bend toward the older country music tradition but later encompassed artists who struck out as independent operators handling their own publishing, recording and performing contracts—all pretty much what Lee Mace and a few others had done years before.

The emergence of the modern country music industry, signaled by WSM's trademark registration of the Grand Ole Opry name in 1950 and, publicly, by the events of 1953, solidified with the founding of the Country Music Association (CMA) in 1958. It received a nod from the general culture in the mid-1960s when city artists started penning tunes like "Nashville Skyline" and "Nashville Cats." The process was completed with the creation of Opryland in 1974.

It is certain that Lee recognized the necessity of making sure his show was musically competitive with the new country style that was rapidly evolving.

The musical makeup of the original Ozark Opry gang was "Monroe Standard" bluegrass, a standard that remains the rule in today's bluegrass groups: banjo, fiddle, mandolin, rhythm guitar and dog house bass. An exception to the standard was Lee's preference for a steel guitar in the lineup.

As noted, country music was a fragmented industry and art form in the 1950s. While many young artists had fallen under the spell of Les Paul or Chet Atkins and, later, the pedal steel guitar, a significant number of artists and audiences were also thrilled with a new style of five-string banjo picking.

On December 8, 1945, a young country lad named Earl Scruggs made his Grand Ole Opry debut playing banjo with Bill Monroe and the Bluegrass Boys. The three-finger picking now known as Scruggs-style banjo immediately captivated audiences.

Scruggs-style banjo is about excitement, no matter what the tempo or tune. And the emergence of the syncopated rolls and percussive backup chords on the banjo—an instrument that generally defied hard wiring to an amplifier—gave new life to the old acoustic country sound.

Although Lee Mace would make several instrument adjustments to the Ozark Opry over the years, for the first decade of the show, it was mostly acoustic and a good part bluegrass.

During that time, from 1953 to 1963, the Ozark Opry had only two banjo players; both played Scruggs style, and both started with the show as teenagers.

10

HAT AND BUCKLE
BLUEGRASS BOY

The first banjo player that Lee Mace hired for the Ozark Opry was seventeen-year-old Lonnie Hoppers from the southwest Missouri Ozarks in 1953. Over a half century later, Lonnie and his wife, Charlene, still live in Hickory County, although these days they winter in the Rio Grande Valley in Texas.

Lonnie's grandfather built their house in Missouri, a sturdy farmstead cottage. Both the Hoppers are from old Ozark families. Charlene, an accomplished bluegrass guitarist, recalled that, in the old days, their grandparents were integral participants in the big regional picnic over in Dallas County, known as the Louisburg Picnic or Old Settlers Reunion. Her grandfather operated the "swing," a horse-powered carousel that he owned as a business, and Lonnie's grandfather provided the music, playing the banjo while riding on the swing.

Following his mother's and grandfather's lead—Lonnie's father played the fiddle and harmonica—Lonnie took up the banjo at age thirteen, learning to play on a plectrum banjo (a standard-size banjo but without the fifth string) with a flat pick.

"It was an advantage," Lonnie Hoppers said. "I learned the left hand real well before I ever tried picking."

Another teenager from nearby Warsaw, Dale Sledd, shared Lonnie's determination to master bluegrass music, at the time studying rhythm guitar, and the two boys spent hours listening to Don Reno, Ralph Stanley and, later, Earl Scruggs records, trying to figure out the intricacies of the picking methods.

Lonnie has fond memories of the Ozark Opry in the early days.

With the Ozark Opry ensemble as regulars, the KRMS programming began to match the only rival radio station in its broadcast area, Springfield's KWTO. The Springfield station had not had the programming uncertainties that Bob Smith's operation had experienced. Headquartered deep in the Ozarks, KWTO had gone country from the start.

"We started getting fan mail," Lonnie noted, still seeming somewhat taken aback by that fact nearly six decades later. "A lot of fan mail."

The fans wanted to see the Ozark Opry gang in person, so Lee Mace and the troupe started doing one-night shows throughout the region at schools and civic clubs.

Joyce Mace remembered that Lee then got the idea to do a live show for the tourists. There was an old racetrack in Osage Beach to which the radio executives brought in a flatbed truck with a little sound system for the stage and played to very sparse audiences. Lonnie Hoppers recalled that "it was set back off the road, and nobody would drive back there. It didn't work."

Undaunted, Lee Mace, Smith and von Gremp zeroed in on the Lakeside Casino building, which was right in the middle of the tourist action. Unfortunately, the room they rented was in a lower level of the building, not readily accessible from the street. Few tourists would brave the trek through the upper level restaurant, even if they knew where the show was to be staged.

It was then that Lee sprang into action, becoming the "barker" for the show, often escorting tourists through the Casino café and gift shop to the show and piloting his Pontiac, with the loudspeaker blaring, all around the dam area on Saturdays shouting the show's existence from the rooftop.

"Lee had seen the potential from the beginning," Lonnie Hoppers said. "He bought the Ozark Opry name from KRMS for $750 sometime during the first year."

The success of the Ozark Opry attracted attention early on. Lonnie recalled meeting the Mabe brothers in 1955. The brothers regularly came to see the Ozark Opry show. They would, in 1959, found the first successful show in Branson, the *Bald Knobbers Jamboree*. Lonnie Hoppers remembered that the Mabes actually tried a show—prior to their Branson venture—at the Lake of the Ozarks for a while.

Also in 1954, Dale Sledd, still a teenager, played his Dobro at one of the KRMS talent shows and was soon hired to join the Ozark Opry cast. Dale would go on from the Ozark Opry to perform as the rhythm guitar player and second tenor with the Osborne brothers. "Sonny Osborne told me that Dale auditioned for them in a hotel room," Lonnie related. "He said they couldn't shake him, no matter what they played, he was right on top of it. Sonny said Dale was one of the best rhythm guitar players they had ever seen."

In 1958, Lonnie was drafted into the army. Dale took his place on banjo with the show. When Lonnie finally mustered out in September 1960, Dale was firmly established on the banjo at the Ozark Opry. Lonnie did not seek to get his old job back. He and Charlene moved back to Hickory County.

Shortly afterward, Lonnie joined musical forces with Dean Webb, soon to be the mandolin player with the celebrated bluegrass group, The Dillards. Also in the band, dubbed the Ozark Mountain Boys, were Bob Penny and Dude Fellows, a fiddle player who would briefly open his own show at the Lake of the Ozarks. The Ozark Mountain Boys were a hit, playing a Saturday night show on the west side of the square in Hermitage, Missouri, and appearing on KOLR TV in Springfield that same day, as well as on the Joplin, Missouri television station on Sunday afternoons. Their sponsor was a local business, Jim Walters Shell Homes—nowadays called "modular homes." It was a good time, and it was good times for the Ozark banjo picker.

The next year, in April 1962, Bill Monroe, with whom Lonnie had played a date in 1957 and had stayed in touch, called with an offer. Monroe had gotten booked in one of the Grand Ole Opry package tours run by one of the top promoters of country music, "Hap" Peebles. Monroe called Lonnie from Omaha, Nebraska, and told him about the tour. He wanted Lonnie to join him. In addition to the Bluegrass Boys, Ray Price and Pee Wee King were on the bill. It was likely viewed as a big deal to be part of a Hap Peebles tour, particularly since Monroe had spent much of his career working small towns and byways on his own.

The first thing Monroe did was to take Lonnie hat shopping.

The Bluegrass Boys became true Bluegrass Boys only after Bill blessed their hat. Further recognition of their status was awarded in the form of a custom-made brass belt buckle—sponsored by The Gibson Company consultant, Doug Hutchens (a Bluegrass Boy himself), the Grand Ole Opry and *Bluegrass Unlimited* magazine—to Bill and the members of the band.

Lonnie Hoppers is a hat and buckle Bluegrass Boy.

Lonnie played banjo with Bill Monroe for about six months. In the end, it was a matter of income. Unlike Lee Mace, who salaried his crew, Monroe paid his musicians by the gig. Other income came from the Grand Ole Opry, which cut checks for each performer individually, and from Decca Records. Owen Bradley, at the time vice-president of Decca's Nashville operation,

Lonnie Hoppers with Bill Monroe, Jimmy Maynard on guitar and Roger Smith on fiddle. *Courtesy Lonnie Hoppers.*

recorded Monroe whenever he could get him and the Bluegrass Boys into the studio. Hoppers remembered Bradley saying, "Anything by Bill Monroe is sure to sell fifty thousand records." Fifty thousand records sold was a very respectable showing for country artists of the time. Lonnie recorded twelve tunes with Monroe.

In 1978, even though they had been steadily employed with AT&T for several years, the Hoppers packed up and moved to Branson. There, Lonnie joined the Horse Creek Band and began a lengthy stand at Silver Dollar City, a thriving theme park.

In 1985, after eight years at Silver Dollar City, Lonnie Hoppers signed on with the Plummer family show—a Branson institution that dates from 1973. The Plummers were more of a mainstream country music operation than the Silver Dollar City venue, and Lonnie found himself alternating banjo with electric bass and guitar on the show. The Plummer family toured extensively in the off-season, and by the end of the 1980s, Lonnie was ready for work closer to home.

Throughout the 1990s, the Hoppers hosted an award-winning syndicated bluegrass show, *Bluegrass Express*, working out of **KYOO** radio in Bolivar, Missouri.

In the mid-1990s, they started a new group, Lonnie Hoppers and New Union, with Charlene on rhythm guitar. They rented a building on Pomme de Terre Lake and packed the house every Saturday night.

In 1998, an old friend, renowned flat-picking guitarist Dan Crary, called and suggested that he and Lonnie record together. In 2000, the pair recorded a CD for Pinecastle Records, *Dan Crary and Lonnie Hoppers and Their American Band*. The album got a solid response, with one track, "I'll Take Hold of My Savior's Hand," topping bluegrass-gospel charts for a month in 2000.

Following two recent tours in Australia, the Hoppers live quietly. Lonnie is a frequent subject of bluegrass bloggers and academics. He will readily show a visitor the RB250 Gibson banjo he played at the Ozark Opry and for many years after. And, if requested, he will bring out the "Lonnie Hoppers Signature" banjo made by Grundy that he currently plays and show how the "Hoppers D Tuners"—his father's invention—work. Several Ozark musicians have credited Lonnie Hoppers with introducing Scruggs-style banjo to the Ozarks, citing his influence on the playing of Ozarkers Doug Dillard and Dale Sledd and recalling many get-togethers with John Hartford and other pickers.

11

MOBILE MARKET

W ithin the space of a couple of years of the Ozark Opry's debut, through the combination of sold-out shows in the Casino café building and Joyce Mace's shrewd money management, the Maces had accumulated enough capital to purchase a plot of land on Highway 54 in Osage Beach. They began planning the construction of an auditorium—a new venue for the show.

Characterizing the couple's relationship to money, Joyce said, "Lee liked to spread it around. I liked to keep it."

Their method of fiscal decision-making was that he would tell her what he wanted to invest in and ask if she had "anything put back." Of course, Joyce, an expert money manager, usually did, but she would say no. He would ask again, and she would accede, tapping the "put back" fund. "I would always say that this will be the last time," Joyce said. "But of course, there was always a next time."

The Ozark Opry building had a flat floor—with the audience looking up at the stage—for its first two seasons, 1957 and 1958, and three hundred folding chairs for seating. Uncertain about how big audiences might be, the Maces waited to put in a sloped, arena-style floor and permanent seating.

But the crowds came in droves to see the hillbilly show at the Lake of the Ozarks. The chair count reached over six hundred most nights once the floor was raised and sloped during the 1958–59 off-season.

In that same off-season, Lee found an old opera house with over eight hundred seats sitting idle in a small Kansas town. So he drove a truck to Kansas and, with the help of his army buddy Jim Logue (the man who repaired the bass fiddle neck in France during the war), unbolted and dismantled the seats and brought the haul back to Osage Beach.

The Ozark Opry
auditorium, 1957.
Courtesy Joyce Mace.

With the addition of a couple hundred fiberglass seats, the auditorium was ready to accommodate the entertainment of over one thousand ticket holders per show. Bolstered by the promotional voltage of the television show Lee had started in 1956 in Jefferson City and the constant touring of the troupe, sold-out shows soon became the norm at the new Ozark Opry auditorium.

For the first time anywhere in America, there was musical entertainment, without a "name" performer, that ran the same content and crew of entertainers on multiple nights each week and played to a packed house most of the time.

The "starless ensemble" show was a concept that not all performers could immediately grasp. Chuck Sowers, one of the stalwarts of the Ozark Opry of the 1970s and 1980s, recalled his surprise the first night on the job. "I had never seen the show, so I didn't understand it. I was thinking nightclub—I thought Lee would be the star and do all the singing and the rest of us would just play behind him. That didn't happen." Joyce Mace recalled that Lee resisted even the addition of his name to the marquee, which she favored as a proprietary measure. Lee finally agreed, she said, sometime around 1960.

In addition to his role as stage master, Lee was constantly on the move, continually promoting the Ozark Opry. That promotion sometimes took ingenious turns and helped boost the Ozark tourism industry in return. An early challenge was the state park. The Lake of the Ozarks State Park had been established as part of Roosevelt's New Deal, primarily to provide employment through the Civilian Conservation Corps. It was originally part of the National Park System and after World War II was gifted to the State of Missouri.

There were campsites in the park, and it was always near capacity in season—and it was right down the road from the Ozark Opry. It would have been a simple enough matter to go into the park and hand out some promotional materials. Lee had been doing that elsewhere in the area for years. But no solicitation was allowed in the park.

In 1960, Carl Williams, Joyce's brother and Lee's potato pilgrimage partner and close friend, opened the first of the supermarkets he would operate in the lake area. Lee immediately recognized the opportunity, and so was begotten the "Mobile Market"—a converted school bus with a compressor to run refrigeration rolling behind it. While solicitation was forbidden in the park, the mobile market was waved right through the gates. And it was a moneymaker. But for Lee, the payoff was greater because every time his driver, Arthur Phillips, made a sale, a flyer advertising the Ozark Opry went into the sack of groceries.

This "promotion-that-pays-for-itself" (and may even make money) was a key concept with Lee. In 1962, for example, he and Joyce signed a twenty-year lease with the owner of a nearby cave where archaeologists from the University of Missouri had uncovered Native American artifacts and burial sites. The owner had tried to attract tourists with mule rides through the cave, but few city folks were interested. Lee and Joyce, however, had a better idea about how to attract tourists. After securing the lease and putting in some concrete walkways and lighting, Lee began advertising the attraction as Indian Burial Cave. Visitors paid a small admission fee to be floated in canoes on an underground stream through the cave, periodically stopping to view the spotlighted graves of long dead Indian braves. Of course, when the visitors alit at the end of the ride, they were furnished with an Ozark Opry flyer or promotional piece.

Lee also had Cliff Campbell, a non-musician Ozark Opry employee, canvassing highways as far away as surrounding states for roadside advertising space. Farmers were offered five dollars a year for the rights to post small advertisements for the Ozark Opry or Indian Burial Cave on their fences or barns. Most of the time, the offer was made and accepted without much discussion.

And few cars left the parking lot of the Ozark Opry without a bumper sticker touting their attendance.

Lee had a simple first rule of business: "I can get to everything I own," he once said, "in fifteen minutes."

The Indian Burial Cave entrance sign. *Courtesy Joyce Mace.*

The Maces were vigorous investors and businesspeople. Over the years, with partners, they built office buildings, condominiums and a mall; they invested in a Howard Johnson hotel, which they called the "roomin' house"; they owned the first trash-hauling business in the Lake of the Ozarks; and they were proprietors of a "wild mouse" and bumper car amusement park, among other things. But Lee also looked beyond the lake to the future of the Ozark Opry. Nashville without a doubt loomed large in his vision.

On October 6, 1960, Lee applied to trademark the Ozark Opry logo and name. On February 20, 1962, the trademark was duly awarded to Lee Mace, DBA Ozark Opry.

Within a year, and again twenty years later, this registration would be a critical component of things to come.

By 1962, Lee and Joyce had plenty to mind in Osage Beach. The Ozark Opry was doing six to eight shows a week, every night but Sunday, from April to October.

The Ozark Opry had maintained a very high retention rate among its cast. With the exception of Lonnie Hoppers, whose departure was mandated by the federal government, most of the original troupe was still on stage as the decade turned. The two Bobs (McCoy and Penny); Don Russell, who had been Porter Wagoner's fiddler before joining the show in the mid-1950s; and Lee were all still at it. Dale Sledd had joined the group about the same time as Russell. Patsy Sledd, née Randolph, had come to the show in the later part of the decade, as had Bud Carter, from 1959 through 1962. Carter would become famous as both a steel player and an innovator of the instrument, the inventor of the "Carter Changer."

The Ozark Opry gang of the 1950s was a remarkably stable ensemble. But at some point, as the decade of the 1960s commenced, Lee began to hear persistent whispers of a walkout. No accessible informants claim to know exactly what happened, but the core performers of the first ten years with the Ozark Opry were, in one way or another, planning to leave the show. An abrupt walkout could have been costly for Lee, as he would have had to scramble to replace performers while losing thousands of dollars in ticket sales. There was also some talk of a breakaway group starting a show to be called *The Original Ozark Opry*. Whether the case or not, that move would have been stymied with Lee's 1962 registration of the trademark.

Lee's solution to the problem of a potential walkout was simple. Each year in the off-season, from the very early days of the Ozark Opry, Lee Mace rummaged through the Midwest searching for talent. Bill "Goofer" Atterberry, who later often accompanied him on some of these quests, remembers going as far as eastern Kentucky and northern Iowa to see performers in church fellowship halls, bars, roadhouses and barn shows.

Lee had also been running talent shows since the KRMS radio days. The contact information of those of interest to Lee was duly taken down and filed away for future reference.

With a phone list of potential Ozark Opry talent literally in his back pocket, Lee began to hire performers to replace any who might leave. At the same time, he said nothing and fired no one. A lengthy war of nerves ensued.

Out of nowhere, new performers began to appear on the Ozark Opry stage—a new guitar player here, a multi-instrumentalist there. In 1962 and 1963, there were four country comedians in the show, Bob "Luther" Leftridge and Bill "Goofer" Atterberry and the original comics, Bob "High Pockets" McCoy and "Bashful Bob" Penny.

By 1963, there was a shadow performer ready to step in for any and all members of the original Ozark Opry cast. "They were really suspicious of us," remembered Darrel Gordon, the Ozark Opry's shadow guitar player and lead singer of that time. "They watched us like hawks."

And, in 1963, it happened. Much of the original and core group quit the show. "Bashful Bob" Penny, Dale and Patsy Sledd, Don Russell and Bob "Luther" Leftridge were suddenly gone from the show. After an attempt at staging a show as the Casino Opry on a dock by the dam, they went to work for Austin Wood, a competitor who had opened up a place down the road from the Ozark Opry.

Some folks said, and it is entirely credible, that it was simply time for the members of the splinter group to go out in the world to seek their fortunes.

The Austin Wood troupe, 1964. *From left*: "Bashful Bob" Penny, Bob Leftridge, Don Russell, Dale Sledd and Patsy Sledd. *Courtesy Lonnie Hoppers*.

Anyone coming of age musically after five to ten years of the tutelage of Lee Mace would have been ready for Nashville. And that's where most of the departures went, and they achieved success there.

In any case, the absence of the original group created scarcely a ripple on stage, or in the audiences, at the Ozark Opry. The shadow performers simply stepped forward and took center stage as if nothing had happened. As examples, Jim Smith, the Ozark Opry's perennial and talented multi-instrumentalist, took over banjo duties seamlessly, and Bill "Goofer" Atterberry, who would make a lifelong career with the show, began to perform more of the comedy routines for which he would become famous.

Of the original Ozark Opry cast, only Dillard Stamper and Bob McCoy remained. And they both stayed on well into the 1960s. At that time, McCoy decided that he had to mind the family business, a farming and commercial enterprise that included a motel, and reluctantly hung up his High Pockets outfit. Stamper told him that he would leave, too, as it wouldn't be the same for him without McCoy.

As for Austin Wood, his operation was the first professional competitor of the Ozark Opry's. Wood was a well-known and liked blind DJ and musician of the Ozarks. In the 1950s, in addition to his radio work, he played community fairs and festivals in the region with a country band called the Austin Wood Show. As a popular DJ, Wood had made solid Nashville connections and, in 1963, opened Austin Wood's Nashville Opry in Osage Beach.

The cover of his show programs proclaimed "WSM Nashville Grand Ole Opry Stars in Person." His business model was different from the Ozark Opry, relying on star power to bring in audiences. In those days, when urban populations—much of the tourist trade at the lake—were not familiar with country music and its performers, the Nashville stars likely had less pull than Wood expected. The show lasted a few seasons, and Wood died of a heart attack in 1967 at the age of forty-six. "We never had the kind of crowds at Austin Wood's that the Ozark Opry got," said Bob Leftridge.

Lee Mace regarded Austin Wood and other music shows sprouting up in the area with a cool eye. About the same time Wood made his entry, another show debuted near Osage Beach, the Country Music Jamboree, featuring the novelty instrumentation of "Fabulous Musical Plumbing." And at various times during the 1960s, there were other competitors in the area with names like the Ozarks Country Jubilee and Country Music Hall, the latter with a revolving stage, a gimmick that Lee would never have allowed. Lee had a few simple stage rules for performers, including never close your eyes when singing and never turn your back on the audience (the latter being unavoidable on a carousel stage).

None of the early competitors survived more than a few seasons. Most seemed to simply not get the Ozark Opry concept and—doomed like lemmings—strove mightily to import Nashville-style "star-driven" entertainment to the Lake of the Ozarks as they went off the cliff.

It wasn't until the 1970s, with the increased popularity of country music, that star-style competitors began to gain traction. But even so, none would ever achieve longevity of even two decades, much less match the Ozark Opry's half century plus. When the Ozark Opry finally closed, the sole remaining music show in the dam area, Main Street Music Hall, had been in business for only thirteen years.

The problem the competitors of the 1960s created for Lee was not that these operators took business from him—it was a rare Ozark Opry performance that was not standing room only—but that he sent business to them. When Lee's operation sold out a show and turned away audiences who were looking for entertainment, many kept on looking and some found one or another of the competition. Lee knew that Wood and the others were the shape of things to come, and he thought it prudent to make the prospect of going head-to-head with the Ozark Opry considerably less attractive.

Having ruled out magnanimity, Lee sought ways to keep the Ozark Opry overflow from going to his competitors. In the early 1960s, folk music was top forty material. A very successful television show called *Hootenanny* featured only folk music. Although Lee was not familiar with the genre, he saw a potential enterprise in it and began to do research.

Lee and Joyce had purchased most of the properties adjacent to the Ozark Opry. The acreage included an open-air summer stock theater, complete with ticket booth, concession stands and bleacher seats, less than a quarter of a mile from the Ozark Opry auditorium. The building housing the stage sat in a hollow with the audience situated on the hillside above. The theater was in good condition, and Lee saw in it a way to carry out a business tactic that would not only pay for itself but would also deprive a competitor of ticket sales.

Lee Mace's Hillbilly Hootenanny, 1964. *From left*: Mildred and Harold Moore, Ida Blue, Dr. Don Zelade, Duane Bechtold, Linda Grayham, Dan William Peek, Ken Peoples and Jerome Wheeler. *Courtesy Joyce Mace.*

Thus, Lee Mace's Hillbilly Hootenanny was launched. During the 1962 and 1963 seasons, Lee paid close attention to the talent show turnout and the folk music trend in the popular and country music markets. Shortly, he assembled the cast for his new show, which would open later in the 1964 season than the Ozark Opry.

Lee had discovered a chiropractor from nearby Eldon, Missouri, presenting Hank Snow to near perfection. From Versailles, also nearby, he had found a trio of high school boys who performed covers of popular folk groups—the Kingston Trio, the Smothers Brothers and so on—and dressed in the chino slacks and button-down shirts that were *de rigueur* for the genre. They called themselves the New Morning Singers. He plucked a gospel-tinged trio, The Singingaires, from the Ozark Opry cast and rounded the troupe off with a young woman from the lake area who sang ballads in the style of Joan Baez. The master of ceremonies for the new show was Duane Bechtold, who was a relative of Lee's.

In the summer of 1964, as the Ozark Opry audience inevitably reached capacity; those still in line for tickets were encouraged to buy ducats for the show just down the road, the Hillbilly Hootenanny. It worked, and in addition, a wider audience of the young, single adults who often group vacationed or worked summer jobs at the lake—schoolteachers, young professionals and college students—found the Hillbilly Hootenanny a show of interest.

12

LINKS TO LEE

When he was a child in Ashland, Illinois, Fred Newell's parents would once a year load up the car and travel to the Lake of the Ozarks. One of the first things they did upon arrival was to go to the Ozark Opry. Eventually they became friendly with Lee and Joyce Mace, and whenever Lee and the Ozark Opry gang played their area, the Newells invited them to their home for refreshments after the show.

In the summer of 1962, when Fred was a teenager, Lee called and asked him if he would like to play guitar with the Ozark Opry. Fred was on summer break from college and readily accepted. He was majoring in music at MacMurray College and was more than ready to put music theory into practice. He liked the experience so much that he asked Lee to give him a full-time job playing guitar. Lee asked what he had been doing, and Fred told him he was going to college but was not enthusiastic about it. Lee said he should go back to college. "You can't work here," Lee told him. "I'll fire you, then you will have to go back to school." Nothing Fred could say changed Lee's position.

Fred went back to school and, after earning a degree in music, became a professional musician. In 1970, he was playing at Christy Lane's nightclub in Peoria, Illinois, when Lee walked in the door. He had come to see Fred.

They talked about Fred's plan to try his hand in Nashville.

"Lee gave me good advice, just like he did when he told me to go back and finish college," Fred acknowledged.

I told him that I wanted to get session work in Nashville. He told me that it would be rough and that if I wanted to do that kind of work, I'd have to stay in town most of the time and be available. He was right about that. Everything he told me about Nashville turned out to be true. He knew the town.

Fred never saw Lee again after that night. But he has thought of him many times, thought about the disappointment of being told to go back to college when playing guitar with the Ozark Opry was so much fun and how right the advice turned out to be. "I never made it known in Nashville that I have a degree in music," Newell says. "But the education made a real difference for me in the profession."

These days, Fred is a successful studio musician and well known as a top hired gun on lead and steel guitar. His lengthy track record stretches over thirty-five years in Nashville and includes NARAS Super Picker Awards for playing on hit songs with everyone from Ray Charles to George Strait and five ACM Awards with the Nashville Now Band. He continues to record internationally and play live dates with top artists.

Had Lee fired Newell, it would have been with a unique phrase. Lee hired saying, "I need you" and fired with, "I don't need you." A few of the less attentive of the let-go missed the meaning and showed up for work the next day, thereby getting fired twice. But being fired did not preclude being rehired. The surest way out the door was to miss a show or to try to do a show under the influence. Lee seldom took a drink and never missed a show. His secret may have been a parsnip and carrot drink that his sister, Lois, a chiropractor, concocted. They called it "the recipe," and Lee was certain of its powers.

Fred Newell, 2010. *Courtesy Fred Newell.*

A study of the links and leads to Lee makes it clear that the Ozark Opry business plan was keyed off of Nashville. As Fred Newell discovered, Lee knew Nashville. If Nashville banned the term "hillbilly," Lee shouted it from the speaker on the roof of his Pontiac. If Nashville promoted "country pop" music, Lee held fast to the traditional country repertoire. If Nashville went rhinestones, Lee put his cast in preppy blazer jackets and white bucks. It was a deliberate plan. No one who knew Lee could doubt this: he always seemed to know exactly what he was doing and why. As someone once said, Lee always thought ten steps ahead.

And he had fun, real fun, with whatever he was doing, whether playing the bass or thinking up business ideas or just talking. Lee knew how to enjoy most everything.

What most people remember about Lee, though, was how principled he seemed, the strength of character he had. Bill "Goofer" Atterberry aptly described this aspect of Lee when he said, "Lee was just Lee. Everywhere he went, whoever he was with, whatever he was doing, he was always the same—he was just Lee."

When informants speak of Lee, their words often take the form of a testimonial. Lee changed many a young person's life for the better. One such person was Art Reed, who played steel guitar with the Ozark Opry from 1956 to 1959. Art met his wife, Faith, on the show; she was the vocalist and went on to graduate from seminary and become an ordained minister. Today, he and Faith operate a musical instrument business, ArtFolk, in Branson. After noting that "Lee could be harsh—he drove a hard bargain but you could trust him for what he said," Art agreed to write of his Ozark Opry experience. These are his words:

> *By the time I was fifteen my schoolwork was in serious trouble and all I wanted to do was play music. One Friday two men came to my high school math class and asked the teacher if they could speak to me. One of them owned a nightclub and the other was putting together a band. They had a regular guitar and lap steel as well. They offered to take me the next day to buy me a stand up steel guitar if I would come work in the new band.*
>
> *For the next year I worked nightclubs and attempted to continue high school; I was in serious trouble but the applause had taken over my life. My grades and my reputation were ruined.*
>
> *Then a strange thing happened! I was preparing to leave my hometown and go to Iowa with a friend. But a member of the Austin Wood radio*

show offered to take me to meet Lee Mace, who owned the Ozark Opry, before I made the final decision to leave town.

We drove to the television station on a Friday evening where Lee's group did a weekly television show. I auditioned and Lee said he wanted to come visit my parents the following Monday.

On Monday I played pool as usual for most of the day until Lee was to come to our house for dinner. During dinner he told my folks that he would like to hire me to play steel guitar on his show and offered to take me with him that evening. My parents gladly agreed.

While driving down the highway in his Cadillac limousine that evening, Lee said something that began immediately to change my life.

"I think you are a pretty good boy. If you will hold down a job during the day, live where I tell you to live and return to school this fall, you can work on the Opry."

At first I was sure he did not know anything about me, but as it turned out he had been in town most of the day checking me out.

That fall Lee took me to meet Leland Mills, superintendent at School of the Osage. Mr. Mills gave me a standing pass so I could leave any day at any time to go on the road shows with the Opry.

Lee and Joyce Mace, 1965. *Courtesy Joyce Mace.*

I hardly had time to breathe during those years. I graduated with honors and have enjoyed studying ever since. Here is the moral of these memories—I was addicted to applause, the applause continued but the crowd changed, and that changed my life.

Remarkable in this story is the fact that, although Lee was only in his late twenties at the time, he was well into a career of mentoring and "changing the crowd" (from denizens of dives and roadhouses to consumers of family entertainment) for numerous young people.

Cathy DeGraffenreid started as an attendant at the Ozark Opry snack bar at the age of fourteen. She became Lee and Joyce's chief administrator and all-around assistant. Cathy told a reporter in 1985, "Of all the people I have known, Lee Mace was probably the one person who could, at the end of each day, look back with the fewest regrets.

Carl Williams added, "Every night when Lee went to bed, he was always planning and looking forward to the next morning."

Ozark Opry, mid-1960s. *From left*: LeRoy Haslag, Brenda Libby, Bill "Goofer" Atterberry, Paulette Reeves, Leo Burlsworth, Mildred Moore, Jim Smith, Pat Pryor and Lee Mace. *Courtesy LeRoy Haslag.*

Lee, it should be noted, was a man of the Ozarks. He had a powerful sense of right and wrong, and he acted on that sense. He packed a handgun in the glove box of his car, and he was known in his younger days to settle matters of honor with cage fight–level fisticuffs.

And honor was tantamount with Lee. Pat Heller, an acclaimed steel guitarist who played with the Ozark Opry in the early 1970s, recalled an incident that attested to Lee's sense of honor. Lee had a squadron of teenagers whose job it was to put an Ozark Opry bumper sticker on every car in the parking lot every night. The troop attacked their mission with considerable zeal. One night, a man, whom Heller believed was an attorney from Chicago, very pointedly and at unnecessarily high volume warned Lee before the show that he would not brook a bumper sticker on his new car (recollected to have been a Cadillac). Lee assured the man that the car would be spared and instructed his employees as such. The man had a cast on one leg and was offered assistance and special consideration in seating. In any case, Lee handled the situation with the courtesy and consideration an Ozarks gentleman would extend to any guest.

After the show, Lee was summoned to the parking lot, where the enraged attorney pointed to his new car, which was literally covered with bumper stickers. Heller's theory is that some person or persons had overheard the man's preshow tirade and taken the liberty of peeling stickers off other cars and sticking them on the attorney's car.

The lawyer accused Lee of complicity in the deed. Suddenly, there were two enraged men in the parking lot. Lee turned to Pat Heller, who made the mistake of following him outside, and said, "Get me a bucket and some soapy water—now!" Heller hastened to comply. "I didn't ask any questions," he said.

When Heller returned with the bucket, Lee took off his blazer (by the 1970s, the Ozark Opry stage ensemble for men included blazer jackets), soaked it in the soap and water and began scrubbing the bumper stickers off the car. After a while, the lawyer said, "That's OK Mr. Mace, that's enough"—to which Lee replied tersely, "I'll tell you when it's enough." He continued to scrub until every sticker was gone. Then he turned to the lawyer and said sharply that when he gave his word on something, it was final and that if the man did not already have a broken leg, he would have broken one for him. With that, Lee stalked back into the auditorium, leaving a shaken, and fortunate, Chicago lawyer to drive away in a sticker-free car.

But Lee is most often recalled as a kind, generous man with a keen sense of Ozark humor. This is humor based on a tall tale device that is just believable enough to possibly be true. Joyce Mace recalled when she and Lee went to a fabric store to purchase a large number of bolts of the red and green gingham she used in the late 1970s to make skirts for the female cast members. As they were leaving, the owner of the store asked Lee what they were going to do with such a large amount of gingham.

"Lee looked at him and said, sincerely, that he used it to sew his own [boxer] shorts and that he hadn't figured out the cut, so he needed a lot of material to work with."

The dry goods purveyor may be wondering to this day if Lee ever figured out the right cut.

David Webb, Lee's nephew, told the story of Lee and his new Jaguar automobile. The story is told somewhat differently by various people. What follows is an amalgam.

Lee decided he wanted to own a Jaguar automobile, a black one, but none could be found in that color. One day, he flew to Kansas City to visit his sister, David Webb's mother, perhaps to help with some work she needed done. While there, he called the Jaguar dealership and was told they had the model and color he was looking for. Lee, dressed in old blue jeans, borrowed his nephew's beat-up Jeep pickup to drive to the dealership. After parking the aged Jeep in front of the showroom, Lee strolled in and asked to take the black Jaguar for a test drive. This request was met with stirrings of alarm among the dealership staff. One staffer was dispatched to get the manager, who soon emerged and, after surveying Lee's clothing and pickup, declined to permit the test drive.

Undeterred, Lee calmly noted that he was probably going to buy the car as he took a credit card out of his wallet. The manager looked at the card and said, "You can't buy a Jaguar with a credit card." Lee suggested that the man check with the card issuer about that. The manager disappeared into his office and reappeared after a few minutes. He handed the card to Lee.

"Mr. Mace," he said, "you can buy anything you want with your credit card."

Lee bought the Jaguar with the credit card. Joyce Mace still has the car.

In recollections of Lee, most men remember him calling them "son," although it usually meant that they were in trouble of one depth or another. But it also may have been more than a figure of speech. Joyce, to this day, sometimes refers to the Ozark Opry cast as "our kids."

And Lee used to summon the cast to shows by calling, "Alright kids, time to go!"

Most of the cast seems to consider themselves in some way a part of Lee and Joyce's extended family. It was not uncommon for members to seek fatherly advice from Lee.

Over the years, Joyce Mace mothered many of the cast. It was not unusual for Lee and Joyce to take in young performers. Joyce remembers taking Patsy Sledd to get her driver's license and waiting up for Steve Tellman to come home from dates and making him a sandwich as they talked about the evening. Joyce still refers to one charge, Dale Henson, as "my Little One." To this day, like most loving mothers, Joyce celebrates the achievements of her large brood of "kids," grieves their losses and helps out when she can.

In 1964, Bill Atterberry felt secure enough in his Ozark Opry job as "Goofer" to start looking to buy a Cadillac. He had his eye on a spiffy 1956 model but was concerned that the public might think that he was "putting on airs." He asked Lee for advice on the subject. Lee was never dismissive of public perception, but he also was never one to discourage enjoyment of the fruits of labor. He was, after all, known for the bass fiddle–shaped swimming pool behind his house and his penchant for purchasing luxury automobiles.

"It's alright," Lee told Goofer with a grin. "Show them they got their money's worth."

LeRoy Haslag, Lee and Joyce's durable fiddler, spoke of what is perhaps one of the most telling stories about Lee. When on tour, the band shared hotel rooms, sometimes packing in as many as five to a room. One night, while LeRoy was just beginning to doze off and before Lee had retired for the night, Lee went over to LeRoy's bed, straightened the blanket and pulled it up to LeRoy's neck. "He tucked me in!" LeRoy recalled. "I was still awake, but I did not make a move."

13

ROSIN THE BOW

LeRoy Haslag is a tall, courtly man born in 1940 and raised on a farm near Loose Creek, Missouri. His great-grandparents had emigrated from Germany in the late nineteenth century, bringing with them a rich musical heritage. Accordions, fiddles and a variety of other instruments blossom in the Haslag family tree.

LeRoy's father, Aloysius, was a fiddler, and his mother, Hildegarde, played the harmonica. At the age of fifteen, LeRoy decided to take up the fiddle, so his father showed him the basics of the instrument. From there, he listened to fiddle records, the old-fashioned thick 78rpm kind, on a windup phonograph and taught himself the tunes.

Within a few years, LeRoy Haslag was fiddling competitively—very competitively. Soon he was entering fiddle contests around the region and often winning.

In 1959, when LeRoy married his wife, Barbara, he was playing regularly with the Maries Valley Ramblers, the house band at the 87 Club, a roadhouse on Route 87.

The 87 Club was a typical venue for country bands of the time, with a few wooden tables, a bar and a plain wooden dance floor. The wall behind the small bandstand was adorned with several small tin signs advertising Stag beer (apparently the beer of choice of many Ozarkers of that time).

It was at the 87 Club that LeRoy Haslag first met Lee Mace. He believes it was 1958. The Maries Valley Ramblers consisted of three guitars (one of them electric), an upright bass and LeRoy on mandolin. Lee came in one night and asked if he could sit in on bass.

Although the Ozark Opry was a determinedly family show, Lee discovered much of the talent he employed over the years in smoke-filled roadhouses and dance halls, where liquor flowed freely and the show was seldom family oriented.

As a young fiddler, LeRoy kept busy, playing in the late 1950s with the C&O Boys (Cole and Osage) and with the Missouri Wildcats on a live radio show run by a DJ named Ron Lutz on KFAL-AM out of Fulton.

Lutz is now well known and loved as the host of *The Rooster Creek Boys*, a Saturday morning radio show featuring mostly local musicians. Lutz tapes the show during the week in a party atmosphere at his home in rural Cooper County. He occasionally has celebrity guests when they are in the area—and if they are in the know about local legends. John Hartford was a *Rooster Creek* guest during his career.

In 1963, Lee Mace called to offer LeRoy a fiddle position with the Ozark Opry. The pay was eighty-five dollars a week. LeRoy accepted the offer and stayed with Lee until 1965, when he decided to enter the state police ranks as a highway patrol officer.

Four years later, in 1969, LeRoy closed his career as a police officer to return to the Ozark Opry stage, where he would remain until 1975, after

LeRoy Haslag with Don Elkins and the Missouri Poorboys. *Courtesy LeRoy Haslag.*

which he became one of the Maces' on-call performers. When a fiddler was needed, Lee and Joyce knew to rely on LeRoy Haslag. LeRoy also put his art to work on the Ozark Opry stage backdrop, painting an Ozark landscape mural. In an interesting plot twist, LeRoy and Darrel Gordon were contestants in the late 1960s on Ted Mack's *Amateur Hour*.

Darrel Gordon went on to a career as a successful real estate developer and served on the Jefferson City Council for a time. He plays guitar and sings on occasion these days.

LeRoy still plays the fiddle at local gatherings and participated in the Ozark Opry's fiftieth anniversary show in 2002. In the late 1990s, though, he was diagnosed with Parkinson's disease and, as he told a reporter in 2004, has difficulty with tasks like buttoning his shirt and tying his shoes. Sign painting is out of the question, but his long, strong fingers can still find the notes on the fiddle fingerboard, and his right hand steadies at the touch of the bow.

As for sign painting, LeRoy passed that skill on to another Ozark Opry alumnus, David Blaser. In a telephone interview from his home in Florida, Blaser revealed that LeRoy taught him the craft of sign painting and said it has stood him in good stead.

Blaser, from Osage Bluff, Missouri, was the lead guitar player with the Ozark Opry from 1966 to 1969. "Toward the end," Blaser said, "when I turned twenty-one, I finally got Lee to stop calling me his 'married seventeen-year-old guitar player.'"

Like LeRoy Haslag, Blaser got his start in roadhouses and saloons, playing guitar in a duo with his father for a few dollars a night. But he soon moved on to play to larger audiences with the Midwestern Gentlemen and Marvelous Mickey and the Rockasonics before moving to the Ozark Opry.

After the Ozark Opry, David retired from music, moved to Florida in 1984 and set up a siding business. In 2006, he and his wife decided to retire. Then the southern Ford automobile dealers ran a drawing: buy a Ford, win a Toby Keith guitar. David bought a Ford and won that Toby Keith guitar. He was photographed for the paper standing by his new Ford holding the guitar. "People had seen the picture and they asked me to play something," he said. "I never sang much, but I figured I should. Everyone seemed to like it."

Nowadays, David Blaser is a regular performer, with his Toby Keith guitar, at the Spirit of the Suwanee Music Park in Florida.

This chapter closes with the story of Aloysius Haslag's funeral Mass. The Haslags are German Catholics living in the Jefferson City, Missouri area, a

The Ozark Opry fiftieth anniversary reunion. *From left*: Helen Russell, Chuck Sowers, David Blaser and LeRoy Haslag. *Courtesy Helen Russell.*

city settled and dominated by that heritage and faith. So all of the seats in the church were filled with mourners bidding farewell to a well-respected member of the community. There is a time in such ceremonies when the family comes forward and surrounds the casket in a final farewell. In this solemn moment, with the exception of subdued weeping, all was silent.

Then came the song of a single harmonica playing "Home Sweet Home," echoing softly through the cathedral as Hildegarde played her husband's favorite tune. LeRoy later recorded his mother playing the tune, which will be part of Haslag family funerals in the future.

14

REPERTOIRE, WARDROBE AND CULTURE WAR

Although Lee would rely more on electric guitars and the drum set in Ozark Opry shows in later decades, he always had a firm grasp on the traditional sound of country music. For example, he instructed his musicians that he wanted to "feel the drums, not hear them." And he had no use for electric bass.

In addition to the instrumentation of the show (drums were added in 1967), Lee knew exactly what he wanted in the Ozark Opry repertoire, and it varied little over the decades.

In the 1950s country music industry, though, there were several different emerging approaches to the audience. There was the new country and western segment, the bluegrass pickers and "rockabilly," which combined the bogeyman words of the Nashville of that day, rock 'n' roll and hillbilly— and it must have set the teeth of Snow, Tubb and the Nashville establishment on edge to hear such a word spoken out loud.

A country music culture war was underway.

In 1954, as his career blossomed nationally, Elvis Presley signed a performance contract with the *Louisiana Hayride* country radio show. At that time, Elvis had parted ways with his manager over the rock 'n' roll element of his music. The manager had insisted that Elvis identify himself as country and suggested that he call himself the "Hillbilly Cat."

In May 1955, Elvis was invited to tour with a show headlined by Hank Snow that included Mother Maybelle and the Carter Sisters and the Duke of Paducah. By then, Elvis had done some touring on his own and was enjoying success with his releases by Sun Records.

The Hank Snow All Star Jamboree was one of the new Nashville "package" shows. In addition to star performers, there was a young talent contingent, among which management had attempted to bury Elvis. The strategy didn't work. At each stop, the audience only wanted Elvis. Mobs of young women rushed the stage and besieged his dressing room. The last straw for the older stars of the tour was in Jacksonville, Florida, where the crowd stopped the show by booing Hank Snow off the stage and calling for Elvis.

The result of that riot, it has been written, was that the Nashville establishment got word out that any performer who stepped on to the *Louisiana Hayride* stage for any reason would be banned from the Grand Ole Opry. There was nothing it could do about Elvis, who was already far beyond reach, but it could get at its rockabilly-loving rival radio show and did.

The country music culture wars were so bitter that in 1975, Roy Acuff was still looking back and naming names. In his introduction to Jack Hurst's book, he wrote:

> *Other country shows died because they tried to go with trends, fads. That was what happened to the Big D Jamboree in Dallas and the Louisiana Hayride in Shreveport. They went with rock and roll, thinking they were hitting the right course, but the fad drifted away, and they drifted off with it.*

For his part, Lee Mace skirted profitably around such battles; the country music culture war went on without him. He stayed true to the old country music tradition, drawing the majority of the Ozark Opry repertoire from what can be aptly called the "American Songbook"—the body of traditional ballads, fiddle tunes and Americana from which the tradition of country music had sprung. Lee did so with certainty, never doubting the tradition or the audience. He insisted that the music be audience friendly. He reminded his musicians often that they were there to entertain people: "You're not playing for other musicians but for an audience."

LeRoy Haslag remembered one time when Lee asked him to play the show out with a "fiddle tune." LeRoy, a master fiddler, chose one his favorites, "Peacock Rag," a somewhat obscure tune known mostly to fiddlers—not a soul in the band was familiar with it. After LeRoy finished playing, Lee beckoned. "Son," he said, "next time play something we all know."

That was Lee's rule—and by all, he meant the band and, to a great extent, the audience. Lee was always in touch with the audience. If anyone in the audience left before the show was over, the box office manager, Cathy DeGraffenreid, had standing instructions to follow them into the parking lot to find out why.

Jig dancing at the Ozark Opry. *From left*: Mary Nichols, Goofer, Belinda (Williams) Phillips, Perry Edenburn, Vickie (Lombardo) Sparkman and Lee Mace. *Courtesy Joyce Mace.*

"I didn't want to do it," she recalled. "But I did."

Lee's onstage attentiveness to audiences was legendary. Joyce Mace remembered the night he spotted a man having a heart attack back in the seventh or eighth row of the auditorium.

> *The people with the man were watching the show. They didn't notice that he was in trouble. But Lee did, and he stopped the show and jumped off the stage to assist the man. That is how closely he watched the audience.*

Lee's knowledge of potential performance repertoire was as keen as his observation of audiences.

"Before each season," Joyce Mace said, "Lee would ask everyone to give him a list of songs they could perform. Then he'd take each list and go down it with a pen. He'd say 'yes' or 'no' right down the list."

Here is a playlist from one of the Ozark Opry's television shows in 1980. With minor adjustments to account for contemporary content and instrumentation, this list could easily have dated from the Ozark Opry of the 1950s:

Eastbound and Down (with twin electric guitars introduction and a blazing banjo break);
Rollin' in My Sweet Baby's Arms;
Faded Love (with twin fiddles);
You're My Man; Salty Dog Blues;
The Happy Go Lucky Guitar;
Wait for the Sunshine;
Everything A Man Could Ever Need;
and as the credits rolled, Boilin' Cabbage Down.

One of the featured tunes was a country standard, "Faded Love." Three were bluegrass. One, the bluegrass-tinted "Eastbound and Down," was from the 1977 movie *Smokey and the Bandit*, and the remaining three were recent, but not too recent, tunes by established country artists Lynn Anderson, Buck Owens and Glenn Campbell. The closer was a traditional fiddle tune.

Lee summed up his thinking on the direction of the Ozark Opry show and repertoire in 1971: "We're not trying to make musical history—there are a lot of people who pick better than us—but we put on a good show."

Another way in which the Ozark Opry was positioned differently from Nashville country music was that the show never featured the flashy costumes or sequined western wear that were popular with country and western artists in the earlier days of the industry. The closest approximations were the shiny smoking jackets that were periodically featured in the middle decades. Only one cast member, with the exception of Goofer, was ever allowed to wear a cowboy hat—an Alan Jackson presenter who was with the show in the early 2000s.

The conceptual progression of the Ozark Opry can be traced through the clothing of the cast. Joyce Mace made most of the women's costumes during the early years; this was true in the Lake of the Ozarks Square Dancer days, when the women's skirts were made from bandannas, and extended well into the Ozark Opry years. In fact, Joyce had a sewing room upstairs in the auditorium.

During the 1950s, the hillbilly performance art concept ruled the stage, with all performers often wearing something to identify them as rustics, the comic characters exaggeratedly so. Toward the end of that decade, the cast began dressing in what could be described as street clothing. Chinos replaced blue jeans, and western-style plaid shirts were not uncommon. This trend continued until the mid-1960s, when all the men began to wear blazers furnished by the Ozark Opry. Joyce continued to create costumes for the women, usually the gingham skirt and layered petticoat associated with square dancing.

"We got to where we could buy the clothes off the rack," Joyce Mace said. "Once we got a call from the credit card company because we had spent so much at JC Penney they thought someone had stolen the card."

At this point, a conceptual change of the Ozark Opry was underway, but the changes were mostly in appearance and a slight broadening of repertoire. The foundation of the show never changed. Lee was careful to preserve the content and intent of the songs and keep the show family oriented and rooted in the country tradition.

By 1978, the process of reinvention that had commenced over a decade earlier was complete. Discussing the show that year, Lee summarized the Ozark Opry's history in a single succinct paragraph:

> *I felt a family entertainment thing would work at the Lake if it was presented right…We used the country theme because the Lake hadn't really been discovered by too many vacationers yet and I believed that people coming down from Chicago and St. Louis expected to see real hillbillies so that's what we gave 'em. But now times have changed, the people have changed and we have changed. We do blue grass, a little rock, comedy, gospel. But I think we would still have to be considered more country than anything else.*

He also mused in another interview that modern young people were "born in a different rhythm then I was," with a heavy bass line and emphasis on the downbeat.

Eventually, by the 1990s the Ozark Opry stage began to take on the appearance of a Vegas- or Branson-style show. The men dressed in tuxedos or western-style formal wear, and the women dressed in custom-made, fitted evening gowns.

15

GOOFER

Astock character in country shows since the days of minstrelsy has been the country comedian. This character was more central to the early Ozark Opry shows than to other country shows preceding it. For the original Ozark Opry show, the hillbilly comedian characters, essentially the entire cast, provided necessary visual support of the performance art aspect of the show.

Country music show comedians are not obliged to the more recently developed stand-up form of comedy performance, in which the comedian develops a proprietary style and strictly guards his or her copyrighted routines. The country comedian uses mostly public domain material, much of which may find provenance in the minstrel era but can be dated with certainty from the days of vaudeville. Country comedians openly borrow from the old vaudeville routines and from one another freely and without concern for ownership of the material.

Bill Atterberry was the country comedian "Goofer" with the Ozark Opry from 1962 to 1997 and from 2002 to its closing in 2005. Today, Bill does both stand-up and country comedy as a solo performer. Atterberry cites the famous vaudevillian and television variety show star Red Skeleton as the source of many of his bits and skits during his long career.

"You take the material," Atterberry stated, "and adopt it to your style and maybe update part of it. And it works."

Vaudeville isn't dead. You can find its timeless routines and pratfalls included in many of today's country shows. And the country comedian character remains, alongside the fiddle, the most durable and unchanged element of the country music show.

Tom Reeves with Goofer, mid-1970s. *Courtesy Joyce Mace.*

The importance of the role of the homespun comic character in the initial and long-term success of the Ozark Opry show is difficult to overstate. In his 2002 book, *Lake of the Ozarks: Vintage Vacation Paradise*, local historian H. Dwight Weaver described the influence of Atterberry's role on the Ozark Opry and the Lake of the Ozarks: "Bill (Goofer) Atterberry…the show's comedian for more than three decades… achieved nearly as much fame as Lee Mace, and his popularity brought many people to the show, as well as to the lake."

Bill Atterberry invented his Goofer character as a teenager. He had grown up on the family farm at the edge of the Great Plains near the northeastern Missouri town of Shelbina.

In the late 1950s, Atterberry and his friend Bob Leftridge began performing music and comedy in their hometown area as "Luther and Goofer." Their routine drew inspiration from the Nashville acts Lonzo and Oscar and Homer and Jethro. They became a local hit and by the early 1960s were appearing on the *Possum Holler Opry*, a television show that began broadcasting out of Quincy, Illinois, on WGEM TV in 1961.

The *Possum Holler Opry*, which broadcast on Sunday at 12:30 p.m., was the top-rated regional Illinois television show for much of the 1960s, and the personal appearances and performances of the cast drew large audiences. The September 2, 1967 issue of *Billboard* magazine reported that a performance by the *Possum Holler* troupe had "recently broke attendance records at the Keokuk Street Fair"—the event of that Iowa town said to be the biggest street fair in America.

Goofer

In 1961, Lee Mace had heard of the young comic duo, and he sent Joyce on a scouting mission.

"I remember it very well," she said, "because he told me it [the performance venue] wasn't far away at all and it turned out to be seventy-five miles away and on some hard roads to travel."

But Joyce made it to the show and, back in Osage Beach, gave Lee a glowing report of the two young comedians.

Thus began Goofer's nearly four decades with the Ozark Opry and his almost quarter-century collaboration with Lee Mace.

"Lee was like a dad to me," Goofer said. "We did a lot of things together—I had my first steak dinner with him."

He explained that he had been raised on a farm and the family custom was to serve modest fare at home; they seldom went out to eat. "So I really didn't know what was all right. We stopped at a restaurant on one of the first trips I went on with Lee and I ordered an open-face hot beef sandwich."

Open-face hot beef is a classic, inexpensive, home-style Ozark diner and café plate. Thin sliced roast beef is placed on two side-by-side slices of white bread with a scoop of mashed potatoes and beef gravy over everything. In the days before fast-food restaurants came to the farmlands, it was a special treat for rural families, particularly the children, to dine out on this meal.

"Lee said no, go ahead and have a steak dinner. He insisted. I wouldn't have done it myself."

In Bill Atterberry, Lee Mace found his sidekick. Like their contemporaries, Johnny Carson and Ed McMahon, Lee and Goofer were a perfect pairing.

At the beginning of their association, Bill was a teenager and Lee was in his mid-thirties—still quite a young man but a very successful show business entrepreneur and a role model for country youth.

The master showman and the young comedian seemed to know instinctively how to work with each other on stage. Lee would direct the audience's attention to Goofer by leaning toward him while holding an arm around the neck of the bass fiddle like it was a lamppost. While doing this, his facial expression would be one of eager anticipation, as if he just knew that what happened next was going to be the most delightful thing he had ever witnessed. And Goofer never disappointed Lee or the audience—mugging, jokes and pratfalls ensued.

The interlinear to the story of Lee and Goofer, though, is best expressed by the fact that Lee never asked Goofer about his routines nor required a rehearsal. This was very much unlike the show's music, which was rehearsed in a grueling all-day-and-half-the-night, two-week session in the basement of Lee and Joyce's house before each season and periodically throughout the season. And, unlike Goofer's comedy, all musical offerings required advance approval from Lee.

Goofer is well remembered for his compositions of parody and humorous songs. An Internet check of country music radio playlists revealed that some of his tunes are still getting airtime.

Well remembered, too, are the routines presented by Goofer and Jim Smith, the deadpanned banjo player for many years with the Ozark Opry. Smith was celebrated for never cracking a smile and was the perfect foil to Goofer's, for lack of a better word, goofiness.

Also well remembered are Goofer's routines with fellow comic Tom Reeves and the dazzling dueling trumpet numbers Goofer performed with Mike Richardson. What sets Bill Atterberry apart from other country comics is his invention of a female alter ego, Aunt Effie, and his multi-instrumental talents. He plays an impressive array of string and wind instruments.

One of the occupational hazards of country comedy is the physical aspect. Pratfall, strictly defined, is a fall on the buttocks. In the course of a career, however, a country comic will fall on just about every part of his anatomy. Bill Atterberry was no exception.

"I had a routine where when I first came on stage, Lee would ask me why I was late, where had I been? And I would say that I had been kissing all the women in the audience. Then Lee would say, is that right? He would ask the audience if there were women who had not been kissed. Several would raise their hand." (Goofer had, in fact, kissed none of them.)

"When that happened, I would get all excited and jump off the front of the stage and go kiss them."

The drop from the stage front to the floor was about three feet or so.

"One night, somebody had spilled something on the floor, or something was slick—I never found out what it was—and when I hit the floor my feet went out from under me and I landed hard. I saw stars and blacked out for a few seconds."

But the intrepid comedian got up and completed the skit. Now in his sixties, Bill Atterberry suffers for the laughs he generated throughout the decades. He has had both hips replaced and has some other trauma-induced arthritic issues. He said it was all worth it, though—he would do it again. And he did. After retiring from the Ozark Opry in 1997, he went solo for several years. Goofer came back at Joyce's request in 2002 and stayed until the final show in 2005.

Goofer

In a remarkable coincidence, Bill Atterberry, now a widower, in recent years moved to a small town in the southwestern Ozarks. To his surprise, he found that his new home was two houses down from his old mate in mirth, Bob Leftridge. Leftridge has had a long, successful career as a country music singer-composer, comic and master of ceremonies, with a lengthy run with the Bald Knobbers Jamboree show in Branson. The two old friends and now neighbors periodically partner up to do charity shows and public appearances.

Apart from the Ozark Opry, Bill Atterberry has been busy doing commercials and shows. He created and portrayed the character Hap Hazerd for the Sunflower Dodge dealer in Olathe, Kansas, throughout the 1990s. The character is said to have had the highest recall-recognition factor in the region, becoming a household name. In the subsequent decade, Atterberry was retained as spokesman for JC Mattress Factory in Jefferson City. Of interest is the fact that, in these commercials, he appeared simply as himself, in a western-style jacket and string tie, with no introduction.

Over the years, Bill Atterberry—Goofer—has become an almost iconic presence in the Ozarks and beyond. Honors abound. In 1987, he was inducted into the Pure Country and Bluegrass Hall of Fame. In 1995, he was honored with the Country Music News Lifetime Achievement Award, and in 2004 the Missouri Country Music Hall of Fame placed him on its rolls.

But reports of honors do not do Goofer's irrepressible wit and good nature justice, although LeRoy Haslag told a story that perhaps does. After Lee purchased his airplane, he flew to distant shows while the band made its way on the Ozark Opry bus. At the end of the show, the band members would draw cards to see who got to ride home in the plane, often the difference between an hour or two and an all night bus ride. High card draws got the plane trip, and it was highly coveted. On one trip to northern Iowa, LeRoy and Goofer won the draw. They were supposed to land in Jefferson City, but the airport was fogged in so they were diverted to Columbia, thirty miles north but equally foggy. Lee was an expert instrument-qualified pilot, though. So with LeRoy seated in the copilot spot, holding a flashlight on the instrument panel, Lee commenced the landing. As the plane descended in the impenetrable fog, Goofer tapped LeRoy on the shoulder and asked, "Hey, LeRoy, how does that 'Our Father' go again?"

"That was Goofer," Haslag noted. "No matter what happened, he could find the humor in it."

16

THE SEARCH FOR TALENT

The remarkable talent that played at the Ozark Opry during its half-century-plus run is little short of awe-inspiring. Billy Ray Latham, an extraordinary banjo player who got his start with the Kentucky Colonels, was with the show for four years in the late 1960s. Chuck Sowers, from Illinois' "Little Egypt" region, is renowned for his work with rockabilly artists Lou Hobbs and Billy Swan. Fiddlers Kelly Jones, Stan Waggoner, Bob Brown, Walt Roberts (the youngest person ever elected to the Oklahoma legislature; he fiddled at his campaign stops), steel innovator Bud Carter, Stan Stidham, Mike Richardson, Charlie De Clue, Frank and Roger Hulett (one of a pair of father and son Ozark Opry players), Howard Hinckley, Christy Moore, Gale Richey, Wendell Craig, Paul Trollinger and many other fine musicians, vocalists and comedians graced the Ozark Opry stage. They came to Lee Mace in a variety of ways. The following is an essay from a 1970s program:

Lee Mace's Annual Ozark Opry Search for Talent
By Lee Mace
Do you sing or play any kind of instrument or know anyone that does? If so you will want to know about our "Ozark Opry Search for Talent."

Each fall for several years now we have been presenting what we call an "Ozark Opry Search for Talent." This is not a contest, there is no entry fee or no prizes. We do not screen the talent and we have lots of professionals as well as many amateurs. This is why this is not a contest as we do want the amateurs to come and take part in the shows to let the people know what they can do and what sort of talent they have. Our Ozark Opry show has always been made up of more amateur talent than it has

Billy Ray Latham at the
Ozark Opry, late 1960s.
Courtesy Joyce Mace.

of people with experience in show business. I, Lee Mace, have trained and made fine entertainers of a lot of young people who had never been on a stage before coming to work on the OZARK OPRY SHOW.

These shows each fall are always on Sunday afternoon starting at 2:00 p.m. They are usually the third Sunday in October and the first Sunday in November. The show runs from six to eight hours, depending on how many acts we have, and has been known to run for ten hours. We try to let each act do at least two numbers and if time permits they can do three or four. We always have lots of entertainers from several surrounding states here to take part in these shows.

Lee Mace continued the Ozark Opry tradition of hosting talent shows throughout his career. These shows were free and open to anyone who wanted to perform. Hundreds of performers of all sorts turned out. This is the reason that, nowadays, thousands of people say that they "played on the Ozark Opry." After a while, the talent shows settled in at two separate huge events in the fall of each year.

Lee with Chuck Sowers's son, David, 1981. In 2000, David was a member of the Ozark Opry cast. *Courtesy Chuck Sowers.*

It is important to be mindful that this practice, dating from the KRMS Sunday talent shows with Lee, was directly contrary to the prevailing practices of the country music industry. The last performer to join the Grand Ole Opry by auditioning was Stonewall Jackson, and that was in the late 1950s. As the Ozark Opry was reaching out to performers, the country music industry was becoming a closed society that favored singer-songwriters, who, for a shot at success, somehow found their way through the maze of gatekeepers and dead ends to get the attention of the corporate star makers.

Not all Ozark Opry performers came through the talent show mechanism; there were times when Lee went to considerable lengths to recruit talent.

A 1970s Ozark Opry program noted that "even during the Opry's off season, from mid-December to mid-February, Lee is never far away from the world of country music, traveling some 30,000 miles each winter to watch other shows and search for new talent."

James Pennebaker was a Texas-born, classically trained musician led astray at the age of eight by the Beatles. "February 1964," he said. "*The Ed Sullivan Show.*"

Now, Pennebaker is an acclaimed and highly respected Nashville-based multi-instrumentalist who has, in recent years, appeared on *David Letterman* playing steel guitar behind John Fogerty. His first time on national television, however, was in 1981 on *Saturday Night Live*, backing up Delbert McClinton.

James has also done a prodigious amount of recording and touring with artists like Grammy winner McClinton, Lee Roy Parnell, Big & Rich and Jimmie Dale Gilmore, among many others. The rest of the time he is an artist relations manager at Fender Musical Instruments Corporation—a natural fit, as he is a longtime proponent of Fender's Telecaster guitar.

Ozark Opry, 1978. *From left, front row*: James Pennebaker, Bill Scroggins, Goofer, Lee, Mary Nichols and Tom Reeves. *Back row*: Jim Thomas, Helen (Lawton) Russell and Steve Tellman. *Courtesy Joyce Mace*.

But in the 1960s, James Pennebaker was a teenager who wanted to play guitar in a rock band. It soon became evident that Pennebaker could not only play any instrument he wanted to, but he could also do it better than almost anyone else. By the time he was out of his teens, he had toured with Delbert McClinton, backed up western swing artist Leon Rausch and recorded with Freddy Fender.

Following a stint at Deb's Danceland in Grand Prairie, Texas, James Pennebaker worked in the house band at Dewey Groom's Longhorn Ballroom in Dallas. Originally Bob Wills Ranch House, the Longhorn was famous for its association with persons of varying notoriety. Jack Ruby was briefly the manager, and punk rocker Sid Vicious once took an onstage punch in the face from an irate patron. But there were happy times, too.

James was still pleasantly ensconced at the Longhorn in the winter of 1978 when Lee Mace walked up during a break and introduced himself.

"He told me he owned a country music show in Osage Beach, Missouri," James recalled. "He had some albums in the car, and some other materials about the show."

Lee told the youthful master musician that he wanted to talk about working at the Ozark Opry. James Pennebaker said that Lee talked of benefits like profit sharing and health insurance, incentives few musicians are offered.

Lee had flown his plane down to the Dallas–Fort Worth area and said he could fly James and his wife up to Osage Beach and back in one day and give them a tour of the auditorium and the lake area.

"I listened to the albums and the music seemed pretty good, so I decided to look into it. I went the first time by myself," James said.

The next day, Lee and James flew to Osage Beach and back. Soon after, both the Pennebakers had taken the flight and tour. And soon thereafter, Lee Mace called to say he had found them a lakefront house on five acres.

James played the Ozark Opry for one season. He looks at it as a kind of rite of passage. It was his first time away from home and his first time in a demanding daily show rather than in a tour or dance band. But he did it and in the process created lasting memories and friendships.

"Steve Tellman and I became friends," James said. "Whenever I was in the area, we'd try to get together. And Helen Russell and I are still in touch occasionally."

James remembered well Lee Mace's practical wisdom:

> One day, Lee, Steve and I were sitting in a coffee shop and Lee looked across the table at Steve and me and said, "You know there is a difference between being just an acquaintance and being a friend." He was pointing out something about our relationship to the two of us. Lee really cared about people, and he was wise.

Steve Tellman died at fifty-four years of age in 2008. He had been with the Ozark Opry throughout his adult life. James recalled:

> When I was playing Branson with Pam Tillis in 2002, I drove up to Osage Beach on a night off specifically to visit Steve and see the Ozark Opry show. It was great to see Joyce Mace again and also say hello to Helen Russell, but I only saw Steve briefly before the show. We'd planned to visit after the show, but he had something come up at the last minute that prevented us from visiting further. I was glad to be able to visit. I learned a lot from my one season with Lee, and I'll never forget it.

For a short time in 1979, Pennebaker returned to the Longhorn. Then a call from Delbert McClinton set him on a touring and recording collaboration with the harmonica master that lasted into the 1980s. Since then, James has worked with the top echelon of Nashville artists, and in 1993 the Pennebakers moved to that city.

OZARK ANNIE

In the beginning, the 1953 season, there were two women in the Ozark Opry cast, Ramona Bullington and Annie Rambo, who played a Minnie Pearl–type character, "Ozark Annie." Their tenures were relatively brief though, and no informant recalled that they did any touring with the troupe. Ramona still lives in Missouri and works in administration at a college. No informants knew the whereabouts of Ozark Annie.

The first female members of an Ozark Opry ensemble to achieve longevity were the Hall sisters—and that is how they are always referred to, as a unit. Glenna and Donna Hall were teenagers in Eldon, Missouri, when they decided to buy a guitar and get into show business. They earned the money to buy the guitar in the time-honored way of Ozarks teens: picking walnuts. During autumn in the Ozarks of their youth, country kids would often sport hands stained a rich brown from handling the black walnuts they gathered in the fall to make some cash-money. The walnuts would then be sold to processors by the hundredweight through the local farmers' cooperative.

In the mid-1950s, the two teens began to enter talent shows and contests, some of which were run by Lee Mace. He asked them if they would like to perform professionally. With permission from their parents, the girls began performing on stage at the Lakeside Casino and traveling with the band to distant shows. They started in the mid-1950s; Glenna was fifteen, and Donna was seventeen.

The sisters once told a newspaper that they had traveled with the Ozark Opry show to fourteen states in one year.

Glenna was quoted in an article in the *Eldon Advertiser* newspaper ("The Hall Sisters Sing Again at Lee Mace's Ozark Opry," November 7, 2002): "It

Ozark Opry, mid-1950's. *From left*: Dale Sledd, "Bashful Bob," Highpockets, Billie Moore, Lonnie Hoppers, the Hall sisters, Dillard Stamper and Lee (foreground). *Courtesy Joyce Mace.*

was fun. There were eight guys in the band and us. We sang country and gospel music together and also did square dancing."

The sisters are now grandmothers, and both live in Eldon. They reunited for the fiftieth-anniversary Ozark Opry show and said at the time that they were considering getting back into show business.

Shortly after the Hall sisters came a memorable young lady, Patsy (Randolph) Sledd. A girl-next-door beauty and talented musician and singer, she had first come to the attention of Lee and Joyce Mace as an eleven-year-old talent show entry. Six years later, she was on the Ozark Opry stage. Patsy Sledd would go on to a long career in Nashville placing hits in country's top 100 in the 1970s. In 1988, she was named the Independent Record Industry's Female Vocalist of the Year. In recent years, she has operated a successful business making costumes for country music artists in Nashville.

Lee and Joyce were adept at finding and mentoring young entertainers. Lee found most female performers at talent shows, but he discovered at least one, Tiffany Taylor (Miller), singing in a bar in Mississippi. She was fifteen years old but with a very authentic-looking fake ID. Lee told Joyce about his find, saying that Tiffany was "too good to be playing clubs."

Having made a discovery, Lee would visit the parents of the teenage musician and assure them that he and Joyce would look out for their child as he or she became a professional musician. And they did.

When the Hall sisters went on tour in the 1950s, Joyce was there to chaperone. The same was true with all the young women who played and sang at the Ozark Opry.

As the 1960s commenced, Paulette Reeves took over as fiddle player and ingénue of the cast. Paulette and Pat Pryor, both young Ozark girls, wowed audiences during the middle of that decade, as would others later: Shirley Bradhurst, Teresa Leggett and Sarah Ferrell.

Most female performers came and went in one season or so. At least four married cast members, and one married a fan.

One of the longest-running female performers at the Ozark Opry was Helen (Lawton) Russell. Helen's first season was in 1977; she had just turned eighteen.

Helen comes from a musical family in Elmont, Kansas. Her grandfather was a fiddler, and her grandmother played the piano. Her mother and father both played guitar. Helen began playing music when she was barely beyond toddlerhood. She learned all the country instruments but was partial to the banjo.

Her teenage years found her playing bluegrass music in a number of venues, banjo contests, dances and grange gatherings and at the Elmont Opry, a monthly show put together by one of the Elmont churches. Performers donated their time and talent, and ticket proceeds went to charity.

As might be expected, Lee and Joyce Mace attended a performance of the Elmont Opry and caught the act of the bespectacled teen, who played Scruggs-style banjo like it was a birthright. They invited her to come down to Osage Beach and play at an Ozark Opry talent show. She did, several times, before she finally neared high school graduation, at which point she began, in her words, "pestering" Lee to put her in the show. After a talk with her parents, he did.

Helen stayed with the show initially from 1977 to 1979. She still has letters that she got from Lee and Joyce thanking her for participating in the talent shows and the end-of-season letters that all cast members received each year thanking them for the season. She also has a photo of her and Rosemary Moser, another teenage girl who shared the stage in those years.

A person of natural sweetness, Helen saved a journal she kept that inaugural year. The last entry covers closing night 1977; she describes her sadness and how she will miss the cast—most of them as youthful as she— especially Rosemary, "my best friend ever."

Ozark Opry, 1993. *From left*: Goofer, Stanley Stidham, Mike Richardson, Dwayne Marshall, Steve Tellman, Roger Hulett, Charlie De Clue, Helen Russell and Shelly Prudden. *Courtesy Joyce Mace*.

In 1978, a young man from Oklahoma attended the Ozark Opry as part of a family reunion at the Lake of the Ozarks. He told a friend who was there that he was going to ask Helen out after the show. His friend said she would likely demur, as he was a tad wild and she was "as pure as cow's milk." She did not protest, however, and even though he lived in Oklahoma, the two found a way to spend time together. They were married in less than a year.

The Russells ran a successful video business for a number of years, but in 1989, after attending an Ozark Opry show, Helen said, "I knew that was it. I wanted to be back on stage."

By chance, she encountered Joyce Mace in a coffee shop shortly afterward and told her that if she needed somebody, to call on her. And Joyce did.

Helen Russell started again with the Ozark Opry in 1990 and played until the show went out in 2005. She is well remembered by audience and cast alike.

"I miss it so much," she said. "When the show closed it was like losing family."

Like Helen, Vickie (Lombardo) Sparkman got her start with the Ozark Opry in the talent shows. The daughter of Joyce Mace's younger brother, Bob, she first performed at the age of five, in a duet with Goofer's son, Brent. As she grew older, she began working the concession stand and then as a teen became part of the bumper sticker battalion, often pleading with Uncle Lee to put her in the show.

"He said no," Vickie recollected. "He said I would have to graduate high school first. He didn't want to see stars in my eyes."

Lee did allow her to guest on the television show a few times and featured her as a guest performer on some of the road shows. It is noteworthy that Lee never had guest artists on stage at the Ozark Opry, staying strictly with the ensemble show. And he only once had an act that came out especially to do numbers. That was in 1964, when the Singingaires, an evangelical gospel trio that Lee took a real liking to, were brought in from the Hillbilly Hootenanny each night to perform a gospel number in each show.

"Lee loaned us a Jeep to make the [eighth of a mile] run and get back to the hootenanny for our next numbers there," Harold Moore remembered. Harold's wife, Mildred, would become a regular on the Ozark Opry stage, and Harold became the promotion manager and bus driver for the show.

Vickie Williams skipped her senior class trip to start singing with the Ozark Opry. The 1979 season was already underway, and Vickie commenced what would be a twelve-year career as lead singer.

Lee had warned Vickie that he would be hard on her because she was family and he wanted no hint of nepotism in her appointment. She had earned it and had to keep earning it. Not to worry, Vickie had a clear, strong, natural singing voice and an appealing stage presence.

But Lee was, Vickie recalled, hard on her. He told her that sometimes he corrected her in front of the cast to help them learn. But what was hardest for the young girl was that she wanted to sing some of the country pop tunes being churned out of Nashville, and Lee would have none of it.

"Before the season, I would give him my list of songs. They were always ones I really wanted to sing. But he would take out his pen and cross off every one on my list."

One season, Vickie, innocently, really wanted to sing Janie Fricke's "Do Me With Love." It was immediately crossed off. There would be no song about "doing" anyone in the Ozark Opry repertoire.

After a couple of seasons, Vickie took to selecting songs from the Ozark Opry record collection (there were several albums by then) and Gannaway classic country VHS tapes, old tunes she knew would pass muster.

"Lee said we shouldn't change the old songs, because they would be something else from what they were meant to be if we did, but we should try to put our personal twist on them."

Vickie's favorite parts of the show were when the cast jig danced and when Lee recited "That Ragged Old Flag."

"My dance partner was always Uncle Lee," Vickie remembered. "I enjoyed that."

Lee always got a standing ovation when he recited "That Ragged Old Flag" as he had done in most shows since about 1981. The piece was penned and recorded by Johnny Cash in 1974 and tells the story of an old man's town square encounter with a stranger who comments on the poor condition of the flag on the courthouse flagpole. This sets off a proud narrative covering most major military encounters the nation has experienced.

Vickie thinks often of Lee.

"There is not a day that I don't apply his advice," she said. "He always said, 'There is no substitute for sincerity; you're only as good as you just were. These folks have taken a night out of their vacations and they can never get that night back. We want to make it the most memorable they've had. We'll never have that same audience again.'"

"Every night when I close my eyes, I'm back on the stage with Uncle Lee," Vickie said. "I'm back at the show again, and Uncle Lee is saying what he always said before the shows—'OK kids, let's go! Time to go!'"

18

ON THE ROAD

On March 21, 1966, the following item appeared in the pages of the *Columbia Missourian* newspaper: "Ozark Opry to play in Centralia— The Ozark Opry will be in Centralia from 8 p.m. to 12 p.m. Saturday in the high school gymnasium. Lee Mace and the group will be sponsored by the Centralia Kiwanis Club."

Centralia is a small town at the fringe of Boone County in the Little Dixie cultural region of Missouri. It is famous for the Centralia Massacre during the Civil War in which "Bloody Bill" Anderson's Confederate irregulars murdered 22 unarmed Union soldiers and shortly thereafter slaughtered another 150 Federal troops who pursued the Anderson band in the wake of the massacre.

A little over a century later, things had calmed down some, and the Ozark Opry was coming to town.

As noted, Lee Mace reached out to audiences using every available means. He was on television before most people in the region owned television sets. He owned businesses for the purpose of cross-promoting his other businesses (the talent shows were superb vehicles for creating a connection with new audiences), and, perhaps most effective, he and the Ozark Opry never stopped touring. The following is taken from the twenty-fifth anniversary Ozark Opry program:

> *OZARK OPRY ON THE ROAD*
> *During the off season, Ozark Opry tours in their modern, air-conditioned bus. The group performs for many fund-raising organizations such as Shrine Clubs, Lions Clubs, Rotary, Kiwanis, JC's, Band Boosters, etc. They also furnish entertainment for conventions, private parties and schools.*

Bill "Goofer" Atterberry recalled that Lee, at each of the fundraisers, always made sure to talk with the organizers and see to it that they were pleased with the financial results of the event. Lee expressed his intentions as "always leave more than you took. I never wanted to go to a town where I couldn't go back again."

Although the touring tapered off some over the decades, it was always a relatively vigorous part of the Ozark Opry during Lee's time. In 1977, for example, the touring started on February 25 and encompassed twenty-five shows by the end of March. The geographic range was from Wisconsin to Kansas, Illinois, Iowa and Missouri. A mix of civic clubs and school organizations sponsored the shows.

The rest of the season averaged about six road shows a month. But the calendar included the taping of three television shows each Wednesday morning and, as the season geared up in April, six to eight shows a week at the Osage Beach auditorium.

Of course, on the road was where what could go awry was most likely to do so. Lonnie Hoppers recalled an Ozark Opry road trip of the 1950s:

Steve Tellman, 1975. *Courtesy Joyce Mace.*

On the Road

Bob Penny never broke character on stage—he was always "Bashful Bob"—
except for one time. We were playing at a high school auditorium somewhere
in southern Missouri, and Austin Wood was there. Lee was going to bring
him out to do a number, so he was back stage. Bob Penny had just bought a
brand-new mandolin, and it was sitting propped against an amplifier over
by where Austin was to enter the stage. Austin was blind, but he would never
accept help getting out on stage. Sure enough, as he came out he stepped right
on Bob's mandolin and cracked the neck. You could hear the wood and strings
crack and snap. Bob was on the other side of the stage and he ran across and
picked up the mandolin, almost cradled it. You could tell he was in shock,
looking back and forth from the mandolin to Austin. He forgot all about being
Bashful Bob. Austin went on and made his way to the microphone without
any idea of what happened. He just went ahead and did his number.

The early tours of the Ozark Opry were accomplished in car caravans.
Lee's big Cadillac was actually a limousine with a chauffeur partition and
facing seats in the rear. Ten or twelve people could ride fairly comfortably
in it. Others in the cast would ride in one or two other cars. The tours were
literally coast-to-coast for the first few years; bookings were fueled by Lee's
extensive contacts in square dance and country music industries. There
were television appearances at stations across the nation. The only part of
America not visited was New England.

One very early tour was a package tour headlined by Porter Wagoner
when he was running the *Ozark Jamboree*. The troupe included the *Ozark
Jamboree* cast, the Ozark Opry, a bluegrass group Lonnie Hoppers had put
together called the Missouri Mountain Boys, Bobby Lord, Tabby West
and Wanda Lee. Norma Jean might have been along on the trip. This tour
traveled the entire Gulf Coast. Bob McCoy got food poisoning in Florida,
and the promoter absconded with the ticket proceeds. Lee had him arrested
in Georgia. "Other than that," Lonnie Hoppers said, "it was a good time."

Bob "High Pockets" McCoy remembered one eventful trip driving back
from a California tour:

We got into Texas late at night, and in those days there were jackrabbits by
the thousands on the plains. They were everywhere, blanketing the highway,
you could see them in the headlights—you never saw anything like it.

Joyce Mace was driving the limousine with Lee, Dillard Stamper and
McCoy riding shotgun. Asleep in the backseat were Clint "Spook" Johnson,

who had replaced the Ozark Opry's original fiddler, Billie Moore and Sonny Newman, who played steel guitar. Stamper was notorious for pranks, and this night was no exception.

Joyce remembered the incident and noted that the rabbits were on the highway at night for the warmth of the pavement. Joyce was driving, probably because she was, in those days, notoriously a night person, often staying up all night.

> *Dillard said that if we could slow the car and sneak up on the jackrabbits, he believed he could catch one, and then we could slide the glass* [of the front seat partition] *back and throw the rabbit in the backseat with Spook and Sonny.*

So they proceeded slowly across Texas, with Dillard periodically getting out of the car to try to capture a rabbit.

"He came real close several times. He would get right up on one and then it would get away."

Fortunately for the sleeping Spook and Sonny, Dillard did not catch a rabbit that night.

But unfortunately for the slumbering pair, a few hours later, the group decided to stop for breakfast and an oil change. Spook and Sonny were still fast asleep, so they left them in the car. They told the garage to just go ahead and put the car up on the lift; the boys would just sleep right through the oil change. Then they went off to breakfast at a nearby diner.

"Spook woke up," McCoy remembered. "And I guess he was still groggy. Anyway, he stepped out of the car" and fell about six feet to the garage floor.

Distance touring changed considerably when Lee began flying planes. Bob McCoy remembered that he and his wife once flew to Bill Monroe's Bean Blossom Festival with Lee and Joyce.

"The cloud cover was thick when we got there," Bob recalled. "Lee asked us to look for openings and said if we found one he would set it down."

McCoy spotted a clear space and pointed it out to Lee. "I immediately regretted it," he said, "because we were suddenly in a steep nose-dive though the clouds, but without the slightest problem Lee landed the plane in a pasture next to the festival stage."

The landing was the talk of the festival. Lee was wearing a red blazer, and Bill Monroe kept saying how much he liked the jacket. Before taking off that day, Lee gave the blazer to Monroe.

LeRoy Haslag, the fiddler much involved in Ozark Opry history, remembered a prison concert of the 1970s:

It was at the women's prison in Tipton. An all-women audience, Lee called for "Green Green Grass of Home." When we finished the tune, I looked out and about half the audience was crying—uncontrollably. But I guess it wasn't a bad choice, it got quite a response.

The tune is a song that was first recorded in the early 1960s by Porter Wagoner and has since been recorded and performed by many artists. It tells the story of a man who dreams of home as he lies in a prison cell awaiting imminent execution.

The correctional facility in Tipton, though, is generally considered a medium-security hoosegow populated mostly with hot check writers, probation scofflaws and persistent petty thieves. There are high chain link fences and razor wire but no death row.

Then there is the story of Goofer, the fat lady and the locker room. There are a number of variants of this tale. This is the way Goofer remembered the incident:

The Ozark Opry troupe was playing a civic club benefit in a high school auditorium and was accorded the use of the locker rooms in the basement of the gym area as their "green room." This was a luxury because at some

Ozark Opry, 1980. *From left*: Mary Nichols, Frank Ellis, Jim Smith, Wendle Craig, Curtis Williams and Jim Phinney. Lee Mace is not shown. *Courtesy Joyce Mace.*

venues the bus was the staging area. The locker room had enclosed toilet stalls and showers. After the show, some of the men took showers. All changed to street clothing, including Lee, who was the first to finish. As Lee was ascending the stairs from the locker room, he met a large, older woman, who asked him where the locker room was. Lee just motioned over his shoulder with his thumb but paused to watch what she was about. The woman hurried down the remaining stairs and stepped into the locker room unannounced. Goofer was standing by a locker row in his underwear. The remaining men in the room bolted for the door. The woman walked in, undaunted, and told Goofer that she thought he was the funniest person she had ever seen. Then she went into one of the stalls, closed the door and continued to rave about how funny he was as she made use of the facility.

Pat Heller's version of the story ends with the notice that when the fleeing men ascended the stairway, they found Lee flat out on a bench in tears with laughter. Goofer could neither confirm nor deny this conclusion as he was still struggling to pull on his pants at the time.

Goofer later discovered that the woman had asked someone where the closest restroom was and was told that the locker room was nearest. He thought her compliments were sincere but that an urgent bladder also may have motivated her visit.

19

ON THE RECORD

When Red Foley's *Ozark Jubilee* first broadcast nationally in January 1955, it did so from the television station in Columbia, hours from its home station in Springfield. The reason, Joyce Mace remembered, was that the station in Columbia was owned by the University of Missouri and had rare technology for a rural area—a "national feed"—because the university broadcast its sports contests live on network television.

In the time before cable and satellite television, mountain homes in the Lake of the Ozarks area would be fortunate to receive even the fuzziest of broadcasts from stations out of Springfield, Jefferson City or Columbia. But television was the hot new medium, and most folks wanted to own one. Prior to the mid-1950s, however, such an appliance in most Ozarks homes would have served no purpose. Lee told a reporter that he and Joyce had bought one at that time thinking they could receive a Kansas City station, but this was not so.

In March 1953, KTTS TV began broadcasting from Springfield, followed by KYTV in October of that year. That December, KOMU TV, the University of Missouri station in Columbia, commenced operations. Not until February 1955 was a station established in the state capital, Jefferson City—KRCG TV, a CBS affiliate.

Country music shows were broadcast locally almost from the beginning of the various stations. On December 26, 1953, KYTV began to broadcast the *Ozark Jubilee* show out of Springfield. As previously noted, the ABC network picked up that show nationally two years later.

In August 1956, the Missouri Farmers Association (MFA) began sponsoring a weekly television broadcast on the Jefferson City station KRCG of the

The exterior of the Ozark Opry auditorium, 1988. *Courtesy Joyce Mace.*

Ozark Opry. The initial deal was for thirteen weeks. MFA would extend its sponsorship for many years, and the Ozark Opry show would run weekly on Missouri stations until 1985.

Over the years, the Ozark Opry broadcast on KMOS TV out of Sedalia and on various specials around the country. On July 24, 1965, *Billboard* magazine reported that "a CBS-owned TV station presented a country music show, *Ozark Opry*...over the Repertoire Workshop program. Produced by KMOX here, the show was aired in five major markets and over ten stations of the Eastern Educational Network."

In the late 1970s, Lee Mace began putting together a comprehensive media plan that included a recording studio, a complete television studio and plans to put together a show for broadcast and cable television.

The first move, in 1979, was to buy a complete recording studio. Lee purchased the business assets of a successful Des Moines, Iowa area operation, Kajac Record Corp. The Ozark Opry had recorded two albums there in the 1970s, including a double album commemorating the show's twenty-fifth anniversary in 1978.

In 1979, Lee began building a complete studio onto the Ozark Opry auditorium. The construction was completed the next year. The balance of the recordings issued by the Ozark Opry show would be done at the studio. By best estimate, including special projects like Lee's guest narration of "That Ragged Old Flag" for the Air Force Command Band of Scott Air Force Base, the Ozark Opry show and Lee Mace recorded about two-dozen records in the course of the show's history.

Lee hired the founder and owner/engineer of Kajac, Harold Luick, to assist with the transition to Osage Beach and put Luick's two lieutenants, Jim Phinney and Bob Parker, on the permanent payroll.

Both men were union session leaders and master musicians in addition to being technically qualified to run the recording studio. Lee would frequently call on their musical skills to punch up the Ozark Opry show. Parker became the first (and only) black member of the stage show. He moved to California in 1982 and now works as a webmaster and musician.

Lee Mace founded a new recording label, Ozark Opry Records. He signed his first artist, Darrell Thomas, to the label in 1979. Jim Phinney recalled that Thomas immediately made the Billboard Country Charts with his tune "Waylon Sing to Mama" (Ozark Opry 894). That Lee knew exactly what he was doing is validated by an unedited interview with an unidentified television journalist in the 1980s. The interviewer is not fitted with a microphone and sits with his back to the camera. Most of the time, his questions are inaudible. In response to one query, Lee said, "The Nashville thing? They go out of their way, really, to write jukebox honky-tonk hits in order to sell a bunch of records at once, and the public has very little choice in what they hear." In a few sentences, Lee summarized the end result of the Nashville country music industry in the late twentieth century. He essentially said that complete control of everything from the creative process to the means of distribution of country music had rendered the audience irrelevant.

From the days of the Grand Ole Opry Square Dancers and the early shared tours and shows, Lee had interacted extensively with the Nashville establishment and knew many of the country stars personally. Over the years, the Ozark Opry had appeared on the same bill with Nashville stars many times. In 1965, for example, the Ozarkers played the Putnam County Fair with George Morgan, Ferlin Huskey and the Grand Ole Opry Troupe. Some of the early recordings of the Ozark Opry were done in Nashville studios.

But it is probable that the success of the first record from the Ozark Opry label set Lee Mace in a different light with the Nashville powers, who had a somewhat proprietary attitude toward the country charts. Lee would, within a short time, receive a letter from Nashville.

Having demonstrated his mastery of the charts, Lee turned his attention to his consummate business, the Ozark Opry. Jim Phinney, who would stay with the Ozark Opry until it closed, did not recall Lee ever again seeking to sign outside artists to the label and remembered that that contract with Thomas was limited to a single project.

Ozark Opry, 1987. *From left*: Trent Crissup, Bobby Brown, Dale Henson, Tiffany Taylor, Tom Hoffman, Vickie, Steve Tellman, Chuck Sowers, Larry Heaberlin and Goofer (reclining). *Courtesy Joyce Mace.*

Lee proceeded very deliberately with his masterful plan, clearly in control of the process. For the first few years, the Ozark Opry recording studio was an in-house audio service. The television shows were dubbed and lip-synced to overcome the problem of inadequate sound generated by the television stations. In addition to this work, the studio produced a new Ozark Opry album every two years or so.

But Lee was far from done. With Jim Phinney as his technical director, he undertook an ambitious media expansion program designed to take the Ozark Opry far into time and space—decades into the future and worldwide.

In the off-season, 1981–82, Lee journeyed to Hollywood, where he purchased a giant video truck, essentially a complete television studio on wheels containing everything except a transmitter.

Beginning in 1984, the Ozark Opry television shows were taped entirely in the Ozark Opry studio using three cameras and a feed to the video truck.

Lee began putting a cable deal together in 1984, a deal that he told Jim Phinney would ensure that the Ozark Opry would be around for a long time on television. Jim did not know the details, but the plan was to syndicate on broadcast and cable television. It could be that Lee was thinking of Al Gannaway and the longevity of the *Country Classics* films.

But 1985 would be the last year of the Ozark Opry on television.

20

LETTERS FROM NASHVILLE

For three days during the 1980 season, Lee Mace performed each night on the Ozark Opry stage, got a few hours' sleep and flew his private plane to St. Louis to catch a commercial flight to Washington, D.C. At the end of the day, he would reverse the process, arriving back in Osage Beach just in time to kick off the show.

"I don't know how he did it," Joyce Mace remembered. "But he was determined to not miss any of the trial."

The trial in question was a legal action brought against Lee, as owner of the Ozark Opry trademark, by WSM, Incorporated. The action sought to enjoin him from using the word "Opry" in the title of the show on the grounds that it infringed on the trademark owned by WSM, Grand Ole Opry.

WSM had registered the Grand Ole Opry trademark in 1950. Lee had registered the Ozark Opry trademark a decade later.

WSM had been slow to react to the hundreds of music operations around the country that used the term "Opry" in their names and then relied on lawyer letters to warn of dire consequences if the word was used. Indeed, one "Opry" owner, Chaisai Childs, told *Billboard* magazine that she had simply written back pointing out that she had performed at the Grand Ole Opry and had at that time been introduced as the "owner of the Grapevine Opry." Why, she asked, had the issue not come up then?

However, according to one authority, by the 1980s, WSM had "a string of court cases" enjoining the use of the word "Opry" and had prevailed in the only two that had gone to trial. There had never been an appeal.

Whatever the case, the corporate counsel at WSM snapped to as the 1980s rolled in and began seeking permanent injunctions against selected

"Oprys." "We can't sue everybody at one time," said a Grand Ole Opry spokesman when asked about the selection process in 1982.

WSM had filed the action against Lee Mace in federal court in Washington, D.C., possibly reasoning that in the midst of his show season, Mace would be more likely to default or give in to its demands. WSM did not know Lee.

Lee showed up at the District of Columbia courtroom, lawyered up and loaded for bear, every day for the first three days of the trial. He had seen WSM coming twenty years away.

Then, somehow, the court became aware of Lee's commuting schedule.

"The judge called them into chambers," Joyce Mace stated, "and said, 'This boy can't be flying out here everyday like this.'"

The judge ordered the parties to reach a settlement of the matter.

Under federal order to come to an arrangement, on May 11, 1980, WSM and Lee Mace agreed that Lee would assign the trademark to WSM in exchange for a fee-free license-back arrangement. Joyce's recollection of the settlement is that the Ozark Opry could operate permanent venues anywhere in the United States, except Tennessee, and tour or do anything else anywhere it wanted under the Ozark Opry banner. WSM could not license the name to anyone else. No money or other consideration was involved, with each party responsible for its own expenses and legal fees in reaching the accord.

Soon after the settlement agreement was reached, dark hints of another intent began to appear. Under a limited assignment of the license, WSM began to assert its rights as licensor.

"They demanded a lot of paperwork, which we gave them," Cathy DeGraffenreid said. "They were supposed to defend the trademark, but they didn't. They just kept making demands."

It seemed likely to the Ozark Opry manager that WSM was looking for a reason to yank the license or at least to bury them in paper and harassment.

In 1970, an Ozark Opry competitor had opened at the Lake of the Ozarks, with a twelve-hundred-seat auditorium: Denny Hilton's Country Shindig. Within a couple of season's, according to court filings, Denny Hilton deduced that potential customers were bypassing his theater because they thought it was some kind of dance show. So, in 1973, he added the word "Opry" to its title: "Dennis Hilton's Country Shindig Opry."

The July 31, 1982 issue of *Billboard* magazine ran a lengthy piece titled "WSM Files Suit Over 'Opry' Use," detailing what eventually happened as a result. At that time, WSM had been granted a temporary injunction against Hilton's use of the word and was demanding that Hilton immediately cease its use and delete it from all promotional material.

The article explored the issues and actions of the parties. In one of the stranger segments of the report, Hilton stated that a person or persons unknown were removing Shindig promotional brochures from the gift shops and tourist spots of the lake area. *Billboard* contacted Billie Berry, co-owner of the Scottish Inn in Osage Beach, who told the magazine that "a man had come in one morning and said he was just looking around and next minute he had taken all our Shindig brochures." The El Dorado Motel, also in Osage Beach, reported the same experience.

The implication was that the mysterious promotion piece purloiners were WSM operatives, but there were other conspiracy theories, too. Hilton said he thought that Lee Mace had alerted WSM to his use of the word, since Lee was his competitor and had a license arrangement with the Grand Ole Opry.

In 1982, Lee Mace was called to testify in the matter. WSM had filed the action in the Kansas City Federal Court, an easy flight from Osage Beach.

A portent of the critical nature of the trial was that WSM brought in some of its stars to testify. They parked a Grand Ole Opry luxury bus outside the courthouse, and Minnie Pearl, Roy Acuff and Porter Wagoner testified about the importance of the word "Opry." Lee had toured with Porter Wagoner and performed on stage with all of them at the Grand Ole Opry and in the Gannaway films. It must have been great courtroom drama.

The drama, however, was greater than a casual observer might have noted. If WSM won the Hilton suit, it was likely that the Ozark Opry was toast, one way or another. On the other hand, if WSM lost, it was the party to be buttered. The trademark and licensing issues would be greatly diminished with the cause of action obliterated.

Hilton's defense had prepared a lengthy review of the etymology of the term "opry." Lee came prepared to put forth the argument he had prepared but never used for his case in 1980. It filled in an important blank. The *New York Times* (John Corry, "Suit Over 'Opry,'" July 15, 1982) reported:

> *Dennis Hilton, a country singer who in 1975 incorporated his performance as "Denny Hilton's Country Shindig Opry Show" is being sued in United States District Court in Kansas City, Mo., to stop using the word "opry." The suit was brought by WSM-AM, which owns the Nashville Grand Ole Opry.*
>
> *WSM says that Mr. Hilton has committed a trademark infringement.*
>
> *Mr. Hilton, however, told Judge Scott O. Wright that "opry" is a descriptive word describing a type of lively show. Meanwhile, Lee Mace,*

a country singer who reached a licensing agreement with WSM so that he could call his show "Ozark Opry" said in court that "infringement is not a good word."

"Confusion is a better word," Mr. Mace said. "I don't know about infringement, but I know about confusion."

And the district court agreed with Hilton and Mace, as did the United States Court of Appeals, Eighth Circuit, on January 12, 1984. The bottom line in the lengthy litigation record is the following from the summation document of the appeals court:

The court stated that the word "opry" is a dialectical variation of "opera," which has been in common use from the eighteenth century to the present, and that "opry" has been and is now used to describe a show consisting of country music, dancing and comedy routines. The court found that the public is aware of the different ownership of the Grand Ole Opry and Dennis Hilton's Country Shindig Opry Show and has exhibited no confusion in distinguishing them.

There is no doubt that Lee's testimony had an impact with the court. Lee's nephew, David Webb, met the judge who initially presided over the Hilton trial—Scott Olin Wright, at the time of that case the federal judge for the Western District of Missouri.

Webb is an auctioneer who runs his auctioning and appraisal business out of Stillwell, Kansas.

I saw an article in the Kansas City Star about the judge's book, and I had gone to court with Lee several times for that trial, even though I was just a child. After the trial we had met the judge, and he told the newspaper that the most interesting case he had in his career was one involving a copyright issue with a man from the Ozarks and the Grand Ole Opry.

The report noted that Judge Wright would be signing his book at a local bookstore that week, and David Webb decided to buy a copy of the book and get the judge to autograph it.

"There was a long line," Webb said. "When I got to the table, I told him that I had met him long ago when I was a child with my uncle, Lee Mace."

The judge looked up at Webb and, smiling, said, "Lee Mace, he was a gutsy son of a bitch."

21

NO STRONGER WILL

It was Sunday, June 16, 1985, and Vickie was visiting her aunt and uncle with her son, Jimmy Joe. Lee joined them for lunch and spent some time with Jimmy Joe. Joyce recalled that as Lee was leaving, he turned around and came back to give Jimmy Joe another hug. Lee seemed quiet, and she thought something was on his mind. He had promised to accompany a local pilot and flight instructor on a pre-purchase flight of a lightweight, experimental aircraft Lee owned. The young man, twenty-four years of age and also named Lee, was planning to buy the open tandem-seat aircraft.

No one can know exactly what happened. Both men were licensed, experienced pilots. The younger man was at the controls. Somehow, the tip of a wing clipped a floating dock. The aircraft flipped several times and went down thirty feet offshore into ten feet of water.

Both men died.

Lee's Mace's funeral was on Thursday of that week. Mildred Moore, one of the Singingaires of the Ozark Opry and Hillbilly Hootenanny, sang "Peace in the Valley" at the funeral. Joyce said that "Lee had once told Mildred that if she outlived him, he wanted her to 'lay that tune on me at my funeral.'"

Goofer recalled that he was overwhelmed at the news of Lee's death. "I went out in the road in front of my house and walked back and forth, I don't know how long. Then I just sat down."

The Ozark Opry was closed as Joyce considered what action to take. Her brothers, John Vernon and Carl, one of Lee's closest friends, urged her to reopen the show. The cast agreed.

"I was hesitant," Joyce said. "I wondered if the men would work for a woman."

June 16, 1985. Lee with grandniece Misty Cochran, grandnephew Jimmy Joe Lombardo (seated) and an unidentified neighborhood child.

Of course, the men had always known that they worked for both Lee and Joyce. And even though Lee was out front on stage, Joyce participated in all decisions. As Cathy DeGraffenreid said in 1985, "Lee always said that Joyce could sing better than most. She had a great ear and could pick out a wrong note immediately. Both she and Lee had a knack for knowing what would work and what wouldn't."

The Ozark Opry extended family rallied around Joyce. Her brothers came by every night to offer moral support, and at Joyce's request, LeRoy Haslag came back as fiddler.

The next Monday, June 24, 1985, the show opened again. What was most touching for Joyce was that much of the community came out to express support. Joyce stood in the aisle and welcomed and thanked each person and family as they filed in to find their seats.

Although the report of Lee's death had been picked up by the wire services and widely broadcast across the nation, some fans did not get the news until they came to the show.

"We had to console a lot of people for a few years," Joyce remembered.

Joyce decided to open each show with a video of Lee reciting "That Ragged Old Flag" and then have the cast come on stage one by one with an "A" chord vamp until they were all on stage.

It was a season-to-season plan. Every year, Joyce considered closing but could not. The show did not close until 2005. Joyce proved to be as capable at adapting, managing and staffing as Lee had been. Joyce was solo at the helm of the Ozark Opry for twenty years of its time in operation. "What she did to go on with the show must have been very hard right after Lee's death,"

Ozark Opry, 2001.
From left: Matt Wallace,
Steve Tellman, Stan
Stidham, Helen
Russell, Matt Gumm,
Tiffany Bryant, Bobby
Brown, David Sowers
and Charlie De Clue.
Courtesy Joyce Mace.

Cathy DeGraffenreid noted. "But there couldn't have been a better way to honor his memory and legacy. I really admire her."

The tours for the rest of the 1985 season were canceled. The Ozark Opry never toured again. The television broadcasts continued until the end of the year with reruns of 1984 shows.

For emcee that season, Joyce recruited Monte Davidson, a popular showman who had had a long running act involving a live bull at one of the luxury resorts at the lake. (Monte made his entrance on the back of the bull—he did not do so at the Ozark Opry).

"We didn't want to hire a Lee Mace impersonator," Joyce said. "Monte was someone we really liked, and he was different, but he did work Goofer to death."

Goofer, accustomed to working with Lee, said that he would often toss the ball to Monte and then Monte would toss it right back. But the transition of styles would have been hard for anyone, Goofer admitted. A succession of emcees followed Monte Davidson. Chuck Watkins, Roger Hulett and Larry Heaberlin each took a turn. All were talented, well-known entertainers, and all were well received by audiences.

Eventually, everyone settled in. Lee had always run the sound system from the stage, but now that fell to Jim Phinney, who set up at the back of the auditorium. Phinney also took the responsibility of assisting Joyce with the recruitment of new talent each year, a process that began in January and needed to be completed by the end of March.

After a few seasons of working to develop a permanent master of ceremonies, though, it was decided that the cast would share that duty. Lee could not be replaced.

22

BRANSON AND BEYOND

It was certainly no accident that the Mabe brothers commenced their Bald Knobbers Jamboree show in Branson in 1959, the year of the dedication ceremony for Table Rock Dam, which would form Table Rock Lake. They and others—notably the Pressley and Plummer families, who also would open shows in the area—had traced the Ozark Opry template perfectly and would build on it.

Table Rock Dam and Lake, along with the long-established tourist destinations of the "Shepherd of the Hills" country and Marvel Cave, duplicated the Lee Mace location criteria exactly in Branson. The rest of the formula was expressed succinctly by the publisher of the Hermitage, Missouri *Index* newspaper, Don Ginnings, in an interview for this book: "Lee Mace was the first to keep the same group on the stage, and change the audience. Now we have a billion dollar a year music industry here in the Ozarks—thanks to Lee."

It is of interest that the Mace template is somewhat malleable. The Carolina Opry in Myrtle Beach has successfully substituted an ocean for a lake and golf venues for caves. Their country comedian is named "Bogie."

Lee's directive not to try to "make music history, just put on a good show," has been universally heeded, as has been the "family" nature of the show's content.

Branson shows are generally "slicker" than were the Ozark Opry productions. Where the Ozark Opry comedy routines and stage presence often had a spontaneous feel, the comedy and staging of the Bald Knobbers Jamboree is orchestrated and precisely produced. It seems unlikely that the timing is ever off. The material and patter are also very professional, as is the

Ozark Opry fiftieth-anniversary group photo. *From left, front row:* Jim Phinney, Steve Tellman, Goofer, Matt Gumm, Joyce Mace, Tiffany Bryant and Steve West. *Second row:* Cindy Wyer, Shirley Prudden, Paulette Reeves, Bobby Brown, Glenna and Donna Hall, Gene Spencer and Larry Heaberlin. *Third row:* David Blaser, Belinda (Williams) Phillips, Roger Hulett, Bob Parker, Chuck Sowers, Howard Hinckley, Helen Russell and LeRoy Haslag. *Courtesy LeRoy Haslag.*

overall production of the Branson shows—lighting and sound are effortlessly maintained, and there are Hollywood-quality special effects, such as stage smoke and the like.

The chief deviation from the Mace template, though, is that the operators in Branson, Missouri, took the family entertainment aspect of the Ozark Opry and ratcheted it up to Christian family entertainment. Where Lee Mace occasionally incorporated traditional gospel tunes into shows, Branson entertainment tilts toward witnessing for the faith. The Bald Knobbers Jamboree Show, for example, ends with an anthem proclaiming Christianity.

Other than as noted, though, the Ozark Opry template remains intact.

It is worth noting that Branson-style venues and music-park shows around the country often sport Ozark Opry alumni or affiliations in their acts. Among them are Clay Campbell of the Kentucky Opry, who as a young man spent many hours with Lee and Joyce; David Blaser, now at the Spirit of the Suwanee Music Park in Florida; Calvin Gilmore, owner of the Carolina Opry, who as a teenager entered an Ozark Opry talent show; and Carolina Opry cast members Dale Henson and Steve Sifford. There are also a number of Ozark Opry grads in Branson, including two superb comedians, Perry Edenburn and Matt Gumm.

But it would be remiss not to spotlight Bob Leftridge. Bob was the "Luther" in "Luther and Goofer" in the early days of the Ozark Opry. He is now the genial and popular master of ceremonies at the Bald Knobber's Jamboree. Bob has made a full circle in his career. After a long run with Nashville's Jerry Rivers that included extensive world tours and song collaborations and recordings, he made his way to the principal Nashville alternative venue, Branson. There he has maintained a vigorous career. In recent years, he has written a book, *The Official Bald Knobbers Joke Book*, done commercials and played frequent solo engagements.

23

OZARK ENCORE

D ecades after the death of Lee Mace, his life and work are still being praised, discussed, analyzed and studied. Lee is legend. He was, for certain, "plumb seldom."

There remains an unanswered question: what is the rightful place of Lee and Joyce Mace and the Ozark Opry in country music cosmology? Their star is fixed in that constellation and should now be acknowledged by the country music industry.

A steady stream of media notice and articles evidence ongoing recognition from the general culture, and the subject of the Ozark Opry is a lively presence on the Internet. In October 2002, Senator Kit Bond read a tribute to the Ozark Opry into the record of the Congress of the United States. In September 2003, a similar honor was accorded as a resolution of the Missouri Senate. It reads in part:

> WHEREAS, it is with special pleasure that the members of the Missouri Senate pause to recognize Lee Mace's Ozark Opry, which is commemorating the resplendent occasion of its Fiftieth Anniversary of operation in beautiful Lake Ozark, Missouri; and...
>
> WHEREAS, Lee and Joyce Mace developed a format for their show that repeats itself night after night to one audience after another for the entire season, a concept that was emulated a few years later in Branson, Missouri, and has spread as far away as Myrtle Beach, South Carolina.

And now there is this tribute to the accomplishment, heart, soul, humor and hard work of two extraordinary people, Lee and Joyce Mace, and to their "kids," the entire cast of the Ozark Opry spanning over a half century.

Joyce Mace and two Missouri legislators with a framed senate resolution. *Courtesy Joyce Mace.*

Lake Ozark Square Dancers, 1953. *From left, back row*: Billie Morris, Spurgeon Atwell, Gene Spencer and Jim Skiles. *Second row*: Tolliver Lawson, Lee Mace, Carl Williams and Dillard Stamper. *First row*: Kathleen Doherty, Joyce Mace, Eileen Williams and Nellie Abbott. *Courtesy Joyce Mace*

Herein is also recognition of the remarkable achievement of the artist-entrepreneurs Tubb, Snow, Acuff and others, all of whom created the modern country music industry and "Music City, USA."

The pioneers of Branson, superb and masterful entertainers and entrepreneurs, are also honored. All have made country music the vast, varied and exciting entertainment that it is today.

CONCLUSION

Performing on Ted Mack's *Original Amateur Hour*, the Lake of the Ozarks Square Dancers begin the dance holding hands, like a maypole circle, moving counterclockwise. The musicians and caller stand still to the right. Then, as the music rises, the dancers drop hands and break into high-energy, individual jigs, still moving with the circle, now clockwise, to the tune and directives of the caller. The audience erupts in thunderous approval, and the dancers seem to become even more animated. They dance for several minutes, changing directions to the call. Male and female dancers moving singularly somehow weave kaleidoscopic patterns, passing and circling one another. The audience is excited and enthralled. As the dance nears its end, the caller, Spurgeon Atwell, a bear of a man, suddenly breaks into dance steps of his own and, still calling the dance, jigs around the moving circle of dancers. Wild cheers and applause ascend from the audience. Spurgeon seems impossibly nimble. As he reaches his place of origin on the circle, the music stops. The applause crescendos. The dancers pause.

SELECT BIBLIOGRAPHY AND REFERENCES

Boulard, Garry. *Huey Long Invades New Orleans: The Siege of a City, 1934–36*. Gretna, LA: Pelican Publishing Company, 1998.

Chiles, Todd H., Alan D. Meyer and Thomas Hench. "Organizational Emergence: The Origin and Transformation of Branson, Missouri's Musical Theaters." *Organizational Science* 15, no. 5 (September–October 2004).

Ginnings, Don. "Ozark Music Industry Began Here: Local musicians Laid Groundwork for Branson Boom." *Index* [Hermitage, Missouri], November 19, 1992.

Hurst, Jack. *Nashville's Grand Ole Opry*. New York: Harry N. Abrams, 1975.

Ketchell, Aaron K. *Holy Hills of the Ozarks: Religion and Tourism in Branson, Missouri*. Baltimore, MD: Johns Hopkins Press, 2007.

Logan, Horace, with Bill Sloan. *Louisiana Hayride Years: Making Musical History in Country's Golden Age*. New York: St. Martins Griffin, 1999.

Malone, Bill C. *Country Music U.S.A*. Austin: University of Texas Press, 1985.

Musick, John Roy. *Stories of Missouri*. New York: American Book Company, 1897.

Pecknold, Diane. *The Selling Sound: The Rise of the Country Music Industry*. Durham, NC: Duke University Press, 2007.

Pugh, Ronnie. *Ernest Tubb: The Texas Troubadour*. Durham, NC: Duke University Press, 1996.

Weaver, H. Dwight. *Lake of the Ozarks: Vintage Vacation Paradise*. Chicago: Arcadia Publishing, 2002.

Wright, Scott O. *Never in Doubt: Memoirs of an Uncommon Judge*. Kansas City, MO: Kansas City Star Books, 2007.

ABOUT THE AUTHOR

Dan William Peek lives with his wife, Joy, in Columbia, Missouri, five minutes from their grandchildren, Grace and Spencer. He has authored a number of articles, essays and reviews on a variety of subjects and a book on the social history of the sport of darts, *To The Point: The Story of Darts in America*. Dan is co-founder and president of Grandparents and Others on Watch, Inc., a nonprofit child advocacy organization.

Visit us at
www.historypress.net